Evangelizing the Culturally Different

Mando Sevillano

© Copyright 1997 — Mando Sevillano

All rights reserved. This book is protected under the copyright laws of the United States of America. This book may not be copied or reprinted for commercial gain or profit. The use of short quotations or occasional page copying for personal or group study is permitted and encouraged. Permission will be granted upon request. Unless otherwise identified, Scripture quotations are from the New American Standard Version of the Bible. Scripture marked (TLB), (NIV), (NKJ), (KJV), and (AMP), are from The Living Bible, the New International, the New King James, the King James, and the Amplified versions of the Bible, respectively. Occasional Scripture emphasis has been added by the author.

Take note that the name satan and related names are not capitalized. We choose not to acknowledge him, even to the point of violating grammatical rules.

Treasure House
An Imprint of
Destiny Image® **Publishers, Inc.**
P.O. Box 310
Shippensburg, PA 17257-0310

"For where your treasure is,
there will your heart be also." Matthew 6:21

ISBN 1-56043-291-8

For Worldwide Distribution
Printed in the U.S.A.

This book and all other Destiny Image, Revival Press and Treasure House books are available at Christian bookstores and distributors worldwide.

For a U.S. bookstore nearest you, call **1-800-722-6774**.
For more information on foreign distributors, call **717-532-3040**.
Or reach us on the Internet: **http://www.reapernet.com**

Special Dedication

As always, for my sons, Paul and Steve,
my daughters, and my grandchildren.

Dedication

To the glory of God alone

Pi God sinmuy amumi pas unanway'kanw kahkawnaqe, oviy pas sukw tiy tavi, nap hak put aw tuptsiwhqa qa hovalniwht, qatsit qaso'taqat himuy'vani (John 3:16 Hopi Text).

For God so loved the world, that He gave His only begotten Son, that whoever believes in Him should not perish, but have eternal life (John 3:16).

"The Spirit of God lies all about the spirit of man like a mighty sea, ready to rush into the smallest chink to fill it."

George MacDonald

Acknowledgments

I wish to thank Dr. Mary Ann Lind, Professor of Asian Studies at Biola University, whose book *Asia: A Christian Perspective* motivated and inspired me to write this book. I subscribe to the notion that its better to repeat a perfectly lucid idea, rather than cloud the issue by attempting to say the idea some other way and reinvent the proverbial wheel. In this treatise, I frequently borrow a word, a phrase, or even a whole passage from Dr. Lind's book. I give full credit for her outstanding work.

I also wish to thank the late Harry C. James for encouraging me to pursue post-graduate studies of the Hopi people and culture more than 20 years ago, and especially for our long conversations at his home in the San Jacinto Mountains. Few people loved the Hopi people and culture as Harry James did. He and Mrs. James entertained and instructed several young Hopi at their mountain home and ranch each summer. He was a frequent visitor to the various Hopi villages for over five decades. He wrote extensively about both the people and culture, and his *Pages from Hopi History* is an authoritative document of the Hopi life.

I express my deep gratitude to many Hopi friends and acquaintances who invited me into their homes, fed me delicious Hopi foods, allowed me to sleep on their roofs on warm summer nights, and shared and explained their experiences with me. Without exception they have requested that their names not be used. This is not merely excessive personal modesty on their parts. First of all, in their eyes, it is very un-Hopi, or *kahopi*, to lift one's self above others. Secondly, like the Hopi of decades past, contemporary Hopi are fully aware that outsiders often have failed to respect their ways, and they have become more self-protective—even secretive—especially in regard to sacred matters. Those of us who respect them and their lifeways have found a people of great warmth, friendliness, a keen sense of humor, and a devout spirituality. I vow to write only true things, for so many wrong things have been said about the Hopi people in the past.

Loren Cunningham, President of the group "Youth With a Mission" in 1985, said in the foreword to Dr. Lind's book that every person upon the face of the earth has two priorities: first, to understand God, and second, to understand one another. Both things must be understood in the light of God's Word. The Bible is the standard by which all cultures must be measured. Every culture has some things that are wrong and some that are right, and it is our job to learn to differentiate between the two.

* * *

No book—especially this one—is the product of one person alone. I have been blessed by the encouragement, support, and prayers of a number of people. To these I am deeply grateful.

I wish particularly to thank Paul and Terri Carruthers, Duane Johnson, and Marion E. Herd for providing me with much-needed information during the preparation of my manuscript.

Finally, I gratefully acknowledge the kindness and helpfulness of J. Koberlein, Elizabeth C. Allen, and Marsha J. Blessing, who assisted greatly in the production of this book.

Contents

	Preface..................... xi
	Introduction xv
Chapter 1	Know Your Role as an Evangelist......... 1
Chapter 2	Learn the Historical Setting of the People.. 11
Chapter 3	Recognize Obvious Biblical Parallels 35
Chapter 4	Learn and Respect the Cultural Context ... 53
Chapter 5	Kingdom Culture Guidelines 77
Chapter 6	Beware of the Leaven of Exotic Religions .. 91
Chapter 7	Know Your Rightful Power in Christ...... 99
Chapter 8	Trust the Spirit of Truth................105
Chapter 9	A Vindication and Apology 113
Chapter 10	Pray for the Nations 121
	Endnotes 127
	Appendix: Reliable and Accessible Hopi Stories......131
	Bibliography 135

Preface

Long ago, even before He made the world, God chose us to be His very own, through what Christ would do for us; He decided then to make us holy in His eyes, without a single fault—we who stand before Him covered with His love. His unchanging plan has always been to adopt us into His own family by sending Jesus Christ to die for us. And He did this because He wanted to! ...And because of what Christ did, all you others too, who heard the Good News about how to be saved, and trusted Christ, were marked as belonging to Christ by the Holy Spirit, who long ago had been promised to all of us Christians (Ephesians 1:4-5,13 TLB).

This treatise is about the evangelization of the nations. Just as Jesus commissioned the early Church to "Go and make disciples in all the nations" (see Mt. 28:18-20), he commissions Christians today to lay spiritual claim to lands throughout the world.

Just before the nation of Israel entered the Promised Land and assumed its spiritual legacy, God instructed Moses to explore the land and to assess the task that lay before them: to go and see what the land was like and what the people who live there were like (see Num. 13:17-18).

Careful exploration (information-gathering) can make the difference between success, labored success, or prolonged near-failure. To present the gospel effectively you must be informed about both the land and its people. Whether directly involved in mission work, called to intercession, or expanding your awareness of the world, you will find this information-gathering to be vital.

Anthropologists and other social scientists define *culture* as "a peoples' entire way of life."[1] Mary Ann Lind gives an instructive slant to this view by defining *culture* as "the acquired ways of behavior [of a people] in a given society."[2]

Since the post-diluvian dispersion of Noah's children from a place in the Near East, and even more so after the post-Babylonian diaspora, cultural differences have characterized all the world's people. The Gospel of Jesus Christ, however, *while often applied within cultural patterns...belongs to no [one] specific culture....*[3] The Spirit of God lies all about the spirit of man like a mighty sea, ready to rush into and fill the smallest chink. The gospel as divine revelation belongs to all cultures, says Romans 1:20. Ever since God created the world, "His invisible attributes, His eternal power and divine nature, have been clearly seen [by all people]."

Our task is not to proclaim the gospel according to our culture but according to God's *Kingdom Culture*. The Kingdom Culture extends beyond the borders of our own experience or even that of the nation, Israel. The Holy Spirit has been moving upon the face of the earth for generations, preparing the hearts of men and women to receive the full gospel. He has been imparting truth since the beginning of time, itself, but the Church continually has closed her eyes to truth not packaged in traditional biblical imagery. If we are to follow the Great Commission, we must step beyond our comfort zones of personal culture and worldview.

Introduction

This book is for the Christian contemplating or already involved with evangelizing a Native American (or any other culturally different people). I hope that my experiences will further prepare him or her for a fruitful ministry.

Kingdom Culture Evangelization calls for a greater sense of commitment to the Great Commission as spelled out in Matthew 28:18-20. We need to develop a conscious awareness of a worldwide fellowship, a *Kingdom Culture,* whose prayer life and activities reflect a genuine commitment and desire to share the gospel in cross-cultural experiences so that all people can be reconciled with God.

This book is not for the close-minded, or those who refuse to engage in the possibility that God's Kingdom is wide enough to encompass groups of culturally different people. It is for the open-minded Christian who hears the call to evangelism and is willing to acknowledge God's sovereignty over His creation. It has been written from a Christian viewpoint, a perspective not limited by science, geography, or culture. The Holy Spirit and God's Kingdom Culture transcend all boundaries.

To be an evangelist among strangers: what a wonderful calling! James tells us that not many of us should become such, for in so doing we will be strictly scrutinized by God. But isn't this proof of His great love for us? Few are chosen. Yet because of this wonderful commission, we are greatly blessed and should be honored to "...endure all things for the sake of those [strangers] who are chosen, that they also may also obtain the salvation..." (see 2 Tim. 2:10).

My field of personal experience involves the Hopi people of Arizona. I have spent more than 20 years as an academic scholar of Hopi people and materials, while living upon reservation land and teaching Hopi students. During that time I faced many unexpected cross-cultural situations and learned a great deal. I have used these experiences and others to introduce the concept of Kingdom Culture and to provide practical counsel for the evangelist, missionary, and teacher.

Spiritually, I believe the Hopi represent one of our great mission challenges. The fire of the Holy Spirit has been kindled upon Hopi lands but has not blossomed yet, for the Hopi have tenaciously held to their traditional ceremonies.

Just as Mary Ann Lind says of the Asians in her book, the Christian perspective sees the Hopi people as:

> an integrative whole in which circumstances of the past, present, and future take on a specific and comprehensive meaning because of a divine blueprint arranged by an omniscient Creator. Such a perspective looks to the Bible for explanations and compassionate responses to today's challenges. [1]

I believe the Scriptures provide a convincing answer to the questions surrounding Hopi religion. They indicate inarguably that the Hopi, (as all other people), have always had the gospel, though perhaps *through a glass darkly*, and are not as far from the knowledge and acceptance of the gospel as some imagine (see 1 Cor. 13:12).

Many points of contact exist for the missionary who will take the time and effort to find them. Today's Hopi religion includes many remnants of God's Word, the *Logos* of the written Scriptures. But to a degree, their hearts have become *darkened*. They, like many other people of the world, have not honored Jehovah God as God and consequently have become *futile in their speculations* (see Rom. 1:21).

(For the sake of clarity, I have used the word, *Truth,* to represent both "Word" and "Light," as synonyms for the Greek word *Logos,* God's total plan [the blueprint for the world]. "Light," in the context of John's writing [see Jn. 1:7], is a metaphor for Jesus Christ, the God-Man and all that He represents. I use the term *Truth,* likewise, as an objective correlative [as T.S. Eliot defines the term]: *Truth* stands for the Incarnation of God as man in Jesus, His Death on the Cross, His Resurrection, Ascension, and the resultant Salvation of mankind, both male and female.)[2]

According to Harry C. James[3], the Hopi are the westernmost of the Pueblo Indians, whose ancestors were the Anasazi or "Ancient Ones," sometimes called the "Cliff Dwellers." During the course of their history, the Hopi have been invaded by the Navajo, the Spanish, the U.S. Bureau of Indian Affairs, the Mormon cult, and anthropologists.

The U. S. government listed the Hopi population as 2,206 in 1887. Today it numbers close to 7,000. Most Hopi live either on the Hopi Reservation proper in northern Arizona or in one of two villages further to the west (Upper and Lower Moencopi) at Tuba City. Some have moved into urban areas such as Phoenix and Los Angeles and have more or less been absorbed into mainstream culture. The

Reservation is entirely surrounded by Navajo lands, as are the two villages at Tuba City. A narrow band of federal property, called the Joint-use Area, separates Hopi lands from Navajo lands. This Joint-use Area was an idea that worked in theory, but both tribes regularly accuse each other of misuse.

Since the Hopi language is essentially a spoken idiom only, (traditional Hopi are reluctant to recognize the contemporary written version), the spelling of Hopi words varies from document to document. Although contemporary scholars have adopted the phonology and spelling systems developed by Professor Ekkehart Malotki of Northern Arizona University, no authoritative complete dictionary of the Hopi language exists at present.

From personal exploration and conversations with local pastors, I discover that five Christian denominations and the Mormon cult have established churches upon reservation land. However, total attendance is small. The oldest—the Mennonite church at Second Mesa New Oraibi, *Kykotsmovi*—has only about ten members. Still the Hopi are politically, economically, and spiritually part of the future, so Christians must take every means possible to develop creative strategies to reach contemporary Hopi as well as other Native American groups with the gospel. Doing this calls for deeply committed people, earnestly praying people, and *an informed people*!

From talking with the Assemblies of God Native American Ministry office, I learn that three million Native American Indians continue to be overlooked in favor of missionary fields in more distant and exotic places. In Arizona alone, the federal government recognizes 22 Indian tribes living on 17 different reservations. The United States recognizes 508 tribes, but only 100 have ever been evangelized. Of the 100 evangelized tribes, 80 percent are being reached by only one full-gospel ministry, the Assemblies of God. During a time when the full-gospel churches (particularly the Foursquare churches) are bombarding the citizens of the 10/40 Window, we simply cannot forget the Native Americans who have done so much for this country and yet received so little in return.

I have highlighted specific principles applicable to anyone working with any group of people with a cultural context other than Euro-American. Some principles fall into the category of cultural awareness, while others are strictly spiritual.

When we look at cultural patterns through Christian eyes, we delight in how imaginative the Creator has been in designing such a fascinating world. When we accomplish spiritual understanding of other people, we thereafter act with greater compassion, consideration, and love toward all people. Cultural differences become opportunities for sharing, not points of separation. We become a part of a much larger eternal culture—God's Kingdom Culture.

Chapter 1

Know Your Role as an Evangelist

For there is no distinction between Jew and Greek [nations]; *for the same Lord is Lord of all, abounding in riches for all who call upon Him; for "Whoever will call upon the name of the Lord will be saved." How then shall they call upon Him in whom they have not believed? And how shall they believe in Him whom they have not heard? And how shall they hear without a preacher? And how shall they preach unless they are sent? Just as it is written, "How beautiful are the feet of those who bring glad tidings of good things!"* (Romans 10:12-15)

Is God calling you to take the gospel, the "glad tidings," to alien cultures? Or is He calling you to be an evangelist to the family next door? Do you think of yourself in terms of evangelist, missionary, or teacher? You may not hold an official title, but all Christians are commissioned to go out in His Name. Life itself is our mission field.

Some believers, however, are specifically called to be evangelists among strangers. What a wonderful calling! Although James says that such believers will be strictly scrutinized by God, (as I stated earlier) isn't this proof of God's great love for us (see Jas. 3:1)? We should be honored to

"...endure all things for the sake of those [strangers] who are chosen, that they may also obtain the salvation which is in Christ Jesus and with it eternal glory" (2 Tim. 2:10).

Regardless of our mission field, we continually face the dilemma of culture. All People see and interpret life differently. This is of concern to the Body of Christ because each denomination or Christian community develops its own cultural boundaries. Crossing these boundaries is often a challenge, even to the most committed Christian. This challenge helps us define our role as evangelists and focus on the exact nature of our ministries.

We are called to share the gospel, not to adjust someone else's cultural attitude. God alone changes the hearts and lives of those who call upon His Name. He sends us to go forth with His Word, in spite of the fact that we might not be comfortable with what we see and hear in other cultures.

Suppose that God calls you to minister to the Hopi society. Are you going to be offended by the matrocentered social structure where family lineage is determined through the wife instead of the husband? Are you going to allow this "minor" point to become a major obstacle to the salvation message? Will your degree of personal offense or your own personal boundaries determine the scope and depth of your ministry, or will you be like Paul? "For I determined to know nothing among you except Jesus Christ, and Him crucified" (1 Cor. 2:2). First Samuel 16:7 tells us not to look at the outward appearance, because God looks at the heart. As evangelists, we are often called to look past the physical and rely upon our spiritual discernment.

God Does Not Show Partiality

God called Saul to serve the very Church he had been persecuting (see Acts 8:1-3; 9:4-6;23-31). Peter had to learn to eat meat (see Acts 10:9-16). Timothy, the son of a Greek, submitted to circumcision (see Acts 16:1-3). Our role as God's ambassador should not be defined by who we are or what religious culture we come from. It should be defined by our willingness to share God's love with all men, regardless of national origin or religious background. God sent Peter to the Gentiles, despite the fact that it was unlawful for a Jew to have contact with them.

And he said to them, "You yourselves know how unlawful it is for a man who is a Jew to associate with a foreigner or to visit him; and yet God has shown me that I should not call any man unholy or unclean." ...And opening his mouth, Peter said: "I most certainly understand now that God is not one to show partiality, but in every nation the man who fears Him and does what is right, is welcome to Him" (Acts 10:28;34-35).

The evangelist must be willing to concentrate on Jesus Christ. Some cultural aspects might be out of line with your understanding of the Scriptures, but bringing men and women to the point of salvation is your primary goal, whether on the mission field, the streets of a large city, or in the pulpit of a community church. Cultural differences are "minor" in comparison to the "major" of presenting Jesus Christ as Savior, Baptizer, Healer, and the Coming King.

We may not be familiar or comfortable with the way people speak, dress, live, and interact with each other. We might not agree with the form of worship, the style of music, or Bible interpretations. One worshiper stands up, while another sits down. He prays loudly while she prefers silence. Some cultures dress with great elegance while others do not dress at all. Will these personal boundaries become gospel barriers?

My experience with the Hopi has taught me to distinquish between majors and minors. I learned to see with a Hopi eye in order to present God's message of salvation. Every time we encounter a new culture, we must learn to see through the eyes of the culture itself. It is my prayer that the things I have seen with Hopi eyes will help people everywhere to reach beyond their personal comfort zones, whether it is with the Hopi people, other Native Americans, overseas missions, the family next door, or the neighborhood church.

The Hopi Mindset

Mindset is a term used by social scientists to indicate "a fixed mental attitude," something that makes it identifiably different from its surrounding neighbors. The missionary must not only be able to recognize his own mental attitudes, but also, he must be willing to acknowledge and respect mindsets of other cultures. Westerners have a mindset: a passion for individual rights and self-aggrandizement. The western community focuses on and encourages individual uniqueness. Children are raised to become "their own persons." Adults dress, communicate, and work in order to "stand out in the crowd."

The Hopi community also has a mindset: Each Hopi is a repository of attitudes shared by his community. Simply, most Hopi tend to think alike. In order to truly communicate, the missionary must understand (or at least be aware of) a fair number of unique Hopi attitudes unfamiliar and occasionally even startling to the non-Hopi. Some unique attitudes include matrilineal kinship, ownership, marriage, and divorce customs.

Matrilineality

The Hopi culture is matrilineal. Lineage and ownership are determined through female (not male) lines. Female relatives, for several reasons, are more important to the individual than male. Not only is one's kinship figured through the female line, but also females own all property. Hopi and western ownership differ, however. Either the oldest female or all the mature female members of the maternal lineage possesses the traditional title to a piece of land, and they alone determine its use.

Matrilineality is a novel idea to the Westerner. In the West, men have always determined lineage, ownership, social status, and family authority. Although the gap is closing, women have had to campaign for basic equal rights.

Marriage

Hopi marriage is lengthy and involved. Many gifts are exchanged between the two families, many rituals are performed over long periods of time, and various other arrangements are made before the couple can formally marry. Betrothed couples live together, under the watchful eye of the matriarch, and children frequently reach the age of five or six before the marriage ceremony is completed. Non-Hopi are sometimes struck speechless at ceremonies where a Hopi bride is presented to the public with two or three children at her side.

When a Hopi man marries, he moves in with his wife, under the roof and supervision of his mother-in-law. He becomes a member of that family, along with all the sisters and their husbands and children. (This reminds the Christian of Genesis 2:24: "For this cause a man shall leave his father and his mother, and shall cleave to his wife....")

Typically, an extra room and other accommodations are added to the mother-in-law's house in order to offer the couple some amount of privacy. The husband, however, continues to consider his own mother's house as his true home. He does not give up his obligations to his mother's household just because he is married. While his mother-in-law's house grows in size and number of inhabitants, his mother's household also grows, for his own sisters marry and bring their husbands to live there.

Although the practice is breaking down under contemporary living conditions, mother-in-law avoidance still is observed by most married men, most of the time. The husband is never alone in the presence of his mother-in-law, and traditionally he does not directly face her if he can reasonably avoid it. (Such sexual avoidance customs are common in other cultures as well.)

Relatives are addressed by kinship terms (even by contemporary Hopi). Using a personal name would be considered disrespectful, reprehensible behavior. Similar deference toward adult relatives is practiced by children in most Christian families today. However, when children reach adulthood, it is often considered an act of endearment to call more distant relatives (aunts, uncles, and cousins) by their given names. The Hopi in general do not use personal names within the family.

When Hopi friends introduce me to family members, they usually speak briefly in the Hopi language and then explain that they must ask for permission to use the personal name. Laughter invariably follows their private conversations.

Divorce

According to Hopi stories, this marriage and living arrangement has functioned successfully since creation. Few things in life, however, are as uncomfortable and potentially unpleasant as the circumstance of a Hopi man whose marriage fails. No alternative is open to him but to "run home to mother." This may not be a great tragedy if the man is still young, for he may be able to find a new wife without difficulty. However, the divorce of a 50-year-old Hopi man can be tragic.

There are no apartments to rent, nor any houses for sale. The man must move back in with his mother, along with his sisters, brothers-in-law, and their children. First, he must face the uncomfortable fact that there is no physical room for him. At night he must seek an available corner not filled with other sleeping mats. Privacy is out of the question. His circumstance is awkward at best. He has become the "sixth finger" of the household. Eventually his family will begin to subtly encourage him to seek a new wife. In addition, his children now belong to the mother's household.

Male/Female Relationships

Hopi often speak of elements, even natural forces, as either male or female. (For instance, there is male and female turquoise, as well as male and female rain.) Anthropologists also speak of male and female sacred activities. While this distinction is often literal denotation, such labels can be metaphoric as well, indicating active and passive experiences. *Hunting*, for example, is "male," while *revelations* of the environment and the cosmos (weather prognostication) is classified "female."

In order to understand the connection between male and female modes of experience and their interconnectedness, we have to consider the Hopi view of gender. Women give birth to babies through internal blood and internal space. To the Hopi, this ability links women with the *earth*, which is the "mother of all Hopi people." (This is literal, not a metaphor to the Hopi).

The ability to give birth confers on women a sense of worth, even though men have complementary power because of their ability to communicate with the supernatural. To the Hopi, the man is merely a seed-planter and does not participate directly in the birth process.

The Hopi man symbolically participates in the creative processes in other ways. In a hunt, for example, men shed blood external to themselves and in external space. In so doing, they create new forms, "giving birth" to skins, fur, and other basic needs.[1] In contemporary times, hunting has become an infrequent (though not extinct) activity, although ritualized hunting remains a regular and vital part of the annual ceremony cycle.

Sacred rituals symbolically depict the male/female, active/passive, internal/external aspects of Hopi life.[2] Hopi men are likened to sparrow-hawks (hunters) and women are likened to butterflies (gentle creatures). In earlier times, young Hopi women wore their hair in traditional butterfly wings (whorls) prior to marriage. These hair whorls, as well as the complete wedding outfit, symbolically embodied the concept of creative potential. Each part of the costume was symbolic and meaningful.

Prayerful cooperation exists between males and females on the individual, the family, the clan, the village, and the phraty (linked clans) level, in order to control the cosmic rhythms of the seasons. Hopi ceremonies are particularly concerned with controlling events, such as rain.

Hopi women "own" (or maintain control over) all farm land, dwellings, cisterns, and the *heart* or "tiiponi" of the main male sacred rituals. All of these are passed on generationally through female kin. Albert Yava, a Tewa-Hopi elder, records:

> The family, the dwelling house, and the field are inseparable, because the woman is the heart of these, and they rest with her...the family traces its kin from the mother, hence all its possessions are hers. The man builds the house, but she repairs and preserves it; the man cultivates the field, but he renders its harvest into the woman's keeping....[3]

The Hopi people have a "sense of place" that is unlike that of Westerners. They possess a profound belief that the Creator made them for Hopiland. There, and only there, is where they rightfully belong. This sense of place is different from and more deeply felt than the wisdom of the aphorism, "home is where the heart is." The Hopi people believe, in a real sense, that the Hopi Way was created for and functions only upon Hopiland.

Do You Have an Open Heart?

Have these cultural distinctions from Hopiland offended you? Is your heart moved to change the way they live or to offer them the Truth (Jesus) that changes the heart of their lives? Your answer to these questions will determine whether or not you understand your role as an evangelist in your local community or abroad. Do not allow cultural prejudice and personal offense to fill your heart with pride and prevent you from being an evangelist for Christ. Lay these things aside and keep your eyes fixed on Jesus alone.

> *Therefore...let us also lay aside every encumbrance, and the sin which so easily entangles us, and let us run with endurance the race that is set before us, fixing our eyes on Jesus, the author and perfecter of our faith, who for the joy set before Him endured the cross, despising the shame, and has sat down at the right hand of the throne of God* (Hebrews 12:1-2).

Chapter 2

Learn the Historical Setting of the People

I planted, Apollos watered, but God was causing the growth…we are God's fellow-workers; you are God's field, God's building. According to the grace of God which was given to me, as a wise master builder I laid a foundation, and another is building upon it. But let each man be careful how he builds upon it. For no man can lay a foundation other than the one which is laid, which is Jesus Christ (1 Corinthians 3:6-11).

When God calls you to the ministry of evangelism, He calls you to take the gospel into the historical context of an individual, group, denomination, or country. The wise counselor knows how past circumstances, events, and struggles have impacted the openness or resistance of an individual or people to the gospel.

Why do nations such as the Hopi continue to resist the gospel? I believe the answer lies in the pages of their history. Hopiland is an excellent reminder that we must learn from the mistakes of the past and build on the spiritual foundations that others have laid before us.

The Summer of 1970

The summer of 1970 marked my first visit to Hopiland. I had driven north from Winslow before sunrise. When I arrived at the crossroads of Highway 87 and Highway 264, at the foot of First Mesa, the only sign of life was a small trading post at the southeast corner of the intersection (78 miles from Winslow, 68 miles from Tuba City, and more than 80 miles from Gallup, New Mexico).

The Turquoise Trading Post's pink walls reminded me of Pepto-Bismol, although its gas pumps (regular and ethyl) were a welcome sight. Inside I found a few basic supplies (soda pop, Hostess Twinkies, and potato chips). A handful of withered produce lay on the shelf, but my attention focused on a sparse supply of *kachina* dolls that had been displayed for the tourists.

Everything was beautiful and wonderful. My heart pounded with excitement and awe at finally arriving at Hopiland. Although I seriously had studied the history and theory of Hopi life, it was only later—after years of reflection—that I realized how truly sparse and bare my observations were that day.

Since then, the Secakuku family has built a fine supermarket a little further to the east, at the bottom of the road that leads up into the First Mesa villages of Walpi, Sichimovi, and Hano. Chief Joe Secakuku's handsome face is pictured on the 1949 cover of *Pictorial America: Arizona Edition.*

Ferris Secakuku was called one of the "short noses," he told me, because of the characteristic bobbed-nose feature of the men in his family. He now manages the supermarket and is very enterprising. When the market first opened, he sent a pickup truck to the mesa-top villages once a week to

Learn the Historical Setting of the People

collect all the ladies who did the shopping. The shoppers were driven down the steep road to the market and, after marketing, were driven back up the hill. Not only was this a clever strategy, but a tremendous boon to the ladies who formerly had to walk the steep hill to their mesa-top homes.

Change Is Not Always Welcome

Some very traditional Hopi did not automatically welcome the market upon their land. To them it was just another intrusion of the modern white man's world into their lives. They recognized the interconnectedness of all things and sensed that the presence of a handy market would change the village forever.

When the Hope Tribal Council met to vote on bringing electricity to the mesa tops in the early 80's, many traditionalists opposed it. The villages of Hano and Sichimovi voted in favor of electricity, but Walpi adamantly voted against it. Before long, however, bright lights were seen in various Walpi windows at night.

A Hopi friend showed me a thick black electrical cord running hundreds of feet along the southern edge of the mesa from Sichomovi to Walpi. He howled with laughter when he said, "Of course, nobody has seen this or knows it's there." Then, he added, "We just pretend not to notice. But you can be sure the clowns will say something about it at the next dance." The *dance* he referred to was the "Home Dance," the last of the sacred *kachina* dances of the season. In this ceremony, the *koshare* or "sacred clowns" teach the people how not to behave by negative example. Lighthearted public shaming is the traditional way of keeping people in line.

Shortly after the electricity incident, a decision to put in a sewer line brought another volley of disagreements between the progressives and traditionalists. A traditionalist believes that a progressive is a sell-out and that his behavior is *kahopi* or un-Hopi. In time, however, a number of houses in Sichimovi (Middle Village) and Hano (to the east) installed flush toilets and showers.

Change Begets Change

Changes of this sort do not modify only the thing itself: All aspects of life connected with that thing are forever different. From a traditional point of view, all of life is upset. The Hopi term for this is: *koyaanisqatsi*, or "corrupted life." "It's not just the way we wash dishes or obey a call of nature," I have heard some of the old people say, "but the old way of life is gone forever."

One cannot deny a certain sadness in this. If Robert Frost's "The Road Not Taken" has taught us anything, it is that there is inherent pain in loss. Whichever road we take, the "road not taken" is forever lost. All change is either progress or decay; all history describes progress or retrogression. Yet, at the human level, one cannot be certain which direction the change will take him.

Change Has Two Sides

Change—even with its inseparable loss—can be viewed from different sides. Those who have integrated electricity and flush toilets into their lives may find it difficult to see a negative corollary to such progress. "It's funny how you get used to such things," one Hopi said.

Hopi society is a tribal society and Hopi people share in ways that Westerners do not. They fulfill traditional roles as members of their families and clans that are unfamiliar to mainstream Americans.

Clan relationships, for example, require specific food-sharing obligations, particularly during certain ceremonies, which could take many days. Certain prayers and other rituals are incomplete (and therefore ineffective) without the participation of both male and female counterparts. Reciprocity, in both the spiritual and ordinary planes of experience, is a key factor of Hopi life.

With the introduction of modern conveniences, many hours that were formerly filled with traditional activities, such as ceremony preparation, corn-grinding, planting, and harvesting, are now unoccupied. These unoccupied hours have all too often been full of destructive activities such as depression and apathy.

While many individuals have been able to successfully turn their leisure time into opportunities for arts, crafts, and other creative pursuits, others have filled their lives with alcohol consumption, television, and malaise. Nearby Tuba City not only has busy health care and education facilities but also has an alcoholic rehabilitation center.

The Gospel Threatens Tradition

Reading the Book of Acts, we Christians do not ordinarily place our sympathies with the Jews who murderously clung to the Mosaic Law. If we did, we would recognize the outrage, pain, and fear that the Jews experienced. They were so threatened by the apostles and the gospel that they were ready to kill any pervader of change in their religious way of life. Since our sympathies lie on the side of the early Christians, it is easy to overlook traditional Jewish fear of change.

Hopi Resistance to Catholicism

The Hopi are also afraid of change. Historically, Catholicism introduced Christianity to Hopiland during the seventeenth century, but it met great resistance. The Roman Church was an arm of the Spanish monarch, with the chief goal of acquiring land and material goods. Records show that the Spanish were genuinely oppressive toward the Hopi, as were they of other Southwest Pueblo Indians.[1]

In 1680 the so-called "Pueblo Revolt" was led by Pope, the Indian religious leader of San Juan Pueblo, New Mexico. This revolt eliminated the Franciscans and all other Spaniards from the Midwest. From the historian's point of view, the results were disastrous: All church and government records were destroyed. Consequently, our knowledge of this revolt has been pieced together from oral sources. (Which are actually trustworthy if coming from an oral-based culture).

Even the Hopi, the "peaceful people," were aroused to violence. At Oraibi (Third Mesa), Father Joseph de Espeleta and Father Augustin de Santa Maria were killed. At the village of Awatovi (now a ruin), Father de Figueroa was killed. At Shongopovi (Second Mesa), Father Joseph de Trujillo was killed.[2]

According to the detailed account of Charles Wilson Hackett, author of *The Revolt of the Pueblo Indians of New Mexico and Otermin's Attempted Reconquest, 1690-1692,* several Hopi remained steadfast to their Christian conversion at Awatovi, but the traditional people tore down the church and converted the priests' quarters for native use.[3]

Mormon Missions

He is the Lord our God; His judgments are in all the earth. He has remembered His covenant forever, the word

Learn the Historical Setting of the People

which He commanded to a thousand generations (Psalm 105:7-8).

The first missionary to contact the Hopi people in 1858 was a member of the Church of Jesus Christ of the Latter Day Saints (Mormon). According to *The Book of Mormon*, the seminal document and basic scripture of the cult, the Americans were one of the "lost tribes of Israel" and had wandered into North America from Palestine some 600 years before Christ. According to *The Book of Mormon*, their dark skin was the result of a curse placed upon them by God because they had neglected His Laws.

Informing people of an alien culture that their dark skin is the result of a curse placed upon them by a God that you are urging them to accept is (at least in contemporary advertising jargon) a poor selling feature! One would assume (quite rightly) that the Hopi were not eager to accept this new God.

Jacob Hamblin, this first missionary, was unsuccessful, so a second missionary, George A. Smith Jr., arrived in 1860. Unfortunately, Smith was shot under mysterious circumstances at a crossing of the Colorado River somewhere inside Navajo land.

The Mormons made a third attempt in 1862 and succeeded because they arrived in Oraibi with food and supplies just after a long drought during which 24 Hopi had died. They persuaded three Hopi to return to Utah with them. During the next ten years Jacob Hamblin continued his missionary efforts, traveling back and forth between Utah and Hopiland.

In 1872, Hamblin finally persuaded a young Hopi couple (Tuva and his wife Pulaskanimiki) to travel with him to absorb the wonders of various industries in several Mormon settlements. The two young Hopi were awed by what they saw; as a result of their report, the Mormons made an inroad. The Mormons established a settlement near the Meoncopi villages where it remains to this day, named after the young Hopi husband—Tuba City.[4]

Although accepted by only a few Hopi, Mormonism has had a greater longevity than any other missionary effort for at least three reasons. First, Hamblin introduced three new food plants to the Hopi: squash, sorghum, and safflower—welcome gifts in a land with a limited rainfall. Second, Mormonism claims that all Native Americans are descendants of the Lamanites, one of the 12 original tribes of Israel. Third, Mormonism states that various Hopi deities are versions of Jesus.

In addition Hopi rules of proper behavior bear a striking similarity to the Ten Commandments. The Mormon cult stresses these imperatives instead of a personal relationship with Jesus Christ.

Although most Hopi reject the Mormon tradition as inaccurate, much of it does harmonize with their understanding of Hopi migration from the Old to New World. As a result, some Hopi claim to follow both the Hopi Way and Mormonism and seem to recognize no problem with their pretension. According to Helen Sekaquaptewa, who claims to be a believer in the Mormon faith, it has been prophesied that the Hopi rituals will one day disappear. In her autobiography, she reported that her father told her the following long before she had ever heard of the *Book of Mormon*:

> There will come a time when the written record will be brought to the Hopi by the white man. There will be many religions taught. You will need to be wise to recognize and choose the right

Learn the Historical Setting of the People

church. It will teach you to be humble and will not try to force you into it. When that time comes we should all forsake our native religion and join this true church. There will come a time when all the people of the earth will belong to one true church. We will all speak the same language and be as one people.[5]

This narrative echoes Philippians 2:10-11: "...that at the name of Jesus every knee should bow...every tongue should confess that Jesus Christ is Lord...."

U.S. Government Tensions Developed

Tension between Hopi traditionalists and progressives is long-seated,[6] in going back at least to 1887, when Superintendent James Gallaher was the first U.S. Government representative to establish an official residence upon Hopi land.

The federal government received a petition signed by 20 Hopi leaders requesting that a school be opened in their country, and Gallaher was ordered to comply with the request. Gallaher, exerting dictatorial powers, made every effort to persuade the Hopi families to send their children to school. However this was a boarding school, requiring that the children be removed from their homes to spend weeks— even months— away from their families.

In addition, a number of Christian beliefs interfered with traditional Hopi ceremonies, which often took days of preparation and called for children to be present for initiations and such. Hopi parents rebelled against Gallaher's rules, so the children were rounded up like criminals and forcibly taken to the government school. This event seriously intruded upon the traditional way of life.

In 1892, with the intention of enticing Hopi families to come down from their mesa-top dwellings, the government built and furnished 26 houses. In 1897-98, a government program for enforced smallpox vaccination wedged the U.S. government even further into Hopi life. The Hopi who supported the government programs were labeled the "friendlies" by Washington, while those opposing were called "hostiles."

Civil War Develops

Tensions between hostiles and friendlies ultimately led to a sort of civil war at Third Mesa Oraibi (the oldest continuously inhabited village in North America). The seeds of discontent germinated and developed into open warfare. Tewaquaptewa, village chief of Oraibi, became the leader of the friendlies. Always a man of peace, he felt that a compromise could be made with the government representatives from Washington—one that would benefit the Hopi people without endangering their integrity. Youkeoma led the hostile faction. The schism came to a head in 1906 during the winter *Niman* ceremony when:

> Youkeoma persuaded about 30 members of a dissident group from another village (Second Mesa, Shongopovi) to join him. Heated argument continued between the factions until late that summer, just before the famed Snake Ceremony was about to be performed. On September 6, meetings were held late into the night and both sides sent men to spy on the other. By morning Tewaquaptewa's group decided to drive the Shongopovi people from Oraibi, and if Youkeoma's people interfered, they would be driven out with them.
>
> Early in the morning, a spokesman was sent three times to ask the Shongopovi people to leave. (By custom, the village chief was not permitted to take a direct part.) They refused. Tewaquaptewa's men seized and threw several out. Youkeoma's men tried to assist their allies, whereupon Tewaquaptewa's men shouted

that they were helping the Shongopovi people. As a result, Youkeoma was seized and bodily removed. No shots were fired during the feud that ensued. Missionaries and government officials stood helplessly at a safe distance.

In the late afternoon of September 8, the village chief and his forces stood on a straight line with their backs to Oraibi, and Youkeoma's forces faced them. Youkeoma stepped across the line toward Oraibi and challenged his opponents, declaring that if they could push him back over the line, he and his followers would leave Oraibi forever. According to some witnesses, Youkeoma took quite a beating, but in the end he was pushed over the line, and the civil war ended.

As the sun had set the hostiles took food and whatever possessions they could carry. Youkeoma led his people to a site with good springs, where they settled in present day Hotevila, the western edge of the mesa villages.

The next day, the superintendent met with Tewaquaptewa and agreed to allow Youkeoma's people to return in groups of no more than three to gather their belongings. During this conference, some people went out to a flat rock where the bloodless battle had occurred and inscribed upon it a straight line—the symbol of Tewaquaptewa's Bear Clan and the symbol of Youkeoma's Masauu Clan.[7]

Christian Missionary Efforts

Toward the end of the nineteenth century and the beginning of the twentieth, missionary activity picked up but with little response from the Hopi people. Some fanatical missionaries were violently opposed to native religious practices, often interrupting sacred ceremonies and destroying holy objects.[8]

Missionaries caused much bitterness by deviously securing land grants from Indian Bureau officials (often through bribes) and building their churches and homes upon Hopi land. Not only was this practice a serious breach of protocol, but also it was a direct insult upon the village chiefs, who represented their local people.

Heinrich R. Voth, a Mennonite missionary and anthropologist, built and established a church at Oraibi in 1901, but because the people became suspicious of his anthropological research activities, he was forced to leave the following year. In 1912, his church was nearly destroyed by lightning, but it was restored and remains in Kykotsmovi (New Oraibi) today.

The Presbyterian church established a mission school at the famous Hubbell Trading Post at Ganado (now upon Navajo land) in 1905. Their objectives included Indian education, health services, and conversion to Christianity, a plan that once again interlocked education with conversion. A hospital later was built there, but the missionary head caused even greater opposition and bitterness because of narrow-minded evangelical zeal. He went so far as to post signs all over Indian land that read: "Tradition is the enemy of progress."

Fanatics, overzealous evangelists, and political opportunists brought the Gospel of Jesus Christ into Hopiland upon the backs of mules, but they were not met with palm branches or hailed for bringing in a new kingdom. However, "...God causes all things to work together for good to [for] those who love God, to those who are called according to His purpose" (Rom. 8:28). Seeds were sown during those early years that are germinating now, and there are Hopi today who are *white for the harvest.* Jesus said, "Behold, I say to you, lift up your eyes, and look on the fields, that they are white for harvest" (Jn. 4:35b).

Learn the Historical Setting of the People

Full-Gospel Missionaries

Full-gospel missions did not arrive at Hopiland until the 1950s. Only the Assemblies of God have managed to maintain an ongoing full-gospel ministry to the Hopi people during the last four and a half decades. By and large, however, the Hopi continue to shun the Christian message. They maintain (or try to maintain) a notable level of secrecy regarding their own native religion and continually apply pressure—primarily through avoidance and covert shaming—against the few Hopi people who have courted or accepted the gospel.

Nonetheless, a steadfast line of Assemblies of God missionaries has served the Hopi people. According to the present pastor, who returned to the Polacca church as interim pastor, there is a line of nine pastors running from the 1950s to the present.

For nearly five decades, dedicated people have risen each morning from their drowsy sleep to light the wick of the gospel. Although their flocks have never been large, and occasionally the light has flickered in the winds of the enemy, the light has never been extinguished. God's grace has prevailed.

Someone once said, "Old missionaries never die; they just change addresses." Though homely in expression, this saying captures both a physical and spiritual truth in the lives of those carrying out the Great Commission. It reflects the pattern that Jesus and His disciples established 2,000 years ago (see Mt. 28:18-20).

Paul and Teri Carruthers

The following scenario is an example of faithful and creative evangelization of a culturally different people. During the early 1980s, Paul and Teri Carruthers were teaching, preaching, and helping the poor at Polacca. As all good workers in the field, they knew that textbook models rarely work. Consequently, they had to innovate in order to meet the needs of their unique congregation. The Carruthers developed a puppet program for the Hopi children, who were delighted because their own native religion incorporates puppetry in some of its sacred ceremony. Teri developed a sewing program for the Hopi ladies, who were already skilled in art and handicrafts of many kinds. (They are, in fact, world renowned in basketry and pottery-making.)

The Carruthers later spent two years on the road with a deputation and evangelistic ministry, and worked for seven years in many villages upon the Papago Reservation, at the Arizona-Mexican border south of Phoenix. They also served upon the Pima Reservation.

Eugene and Naomi Herd

Another example of faithful and creative work is that of the Herds. Altogether, the Herds spent 34 years in Indian missions among and near the Hopi people. The Lord gave Naomi Herd the foresight to write detailed accounts of their lives during the 15 years they spent in the border town of Gallup, New Mexico, where they held weekly meetings at the Hopi villages.

For some well-meaning people, theology is merely a map, with lots and lots of lines outlining all the boundaries of good behavior. Missionaries working in the field among people very unlike themselves quickly discover a lack of clear lines. The Herds found that bending the rules, changing the markers, and making many other adjustments to be axiomatic—not to the gospel, but to the familiar ways of sharing it.

Learn the Historical Setting of the People

Mrs. Herd told me the story of Homer Vance of Shongopovi, who had worked with the movie industry in Hollywood for 50 years. When he quit his work and came home to Hopiland, he actively encouraged his people to "Follow the white man's God." He was known as the "Snake Priest." The Herds developed a loyal friendship with the Snake Priest, and his wife became a follower of Christ. The old man refused to accept Christ until his last moments upon his deathbed.

In 1958, when the Herds left Kansas with their children to set up a home and mission in Hopiland, off-reservation America was reeling from the technological superiority of the Russians, who had put "Sputnik" into orbit—a fact that both angered and frightened the nation. In those days the Russians were referred to as "those Godless communists." During this time the phrase "under God" was added to our Pledge of Allegiance to distinguish us from "those Godless communists." Public education scrambled to find qualified teachers for the Russian language. Only a tiny remnant of God's people had time for a mere 7,000 Hopi Indians living in an area of southern Arizona.

But the Lord cared! The Herds checked in at the Hopi Tribal Headquarters in Keams Canyon, then nestled into their home at Polacca. On top of First Mesa are the three villages of Walpi, Sichmovi, and Hano. Hano village is inhabited by people of the Tewa tribe, who came to live with the Hopi "A little over two hundred and seventy-five years ago," according to Albert Yava, a Tewa born in 1888.[9]

The Tewa people of Hano village moved to the top of the mesa after making an agreement with Hopi to help defend them against other marauding Indian tribes—primarily the Navajo, who had earlier practiced a "hit-and-run" technique

Evangelizing the Culturally Different

of attack. Over the years, however, the Hano and the Hopi have blended culturally, although each maintains its own language and some separate religious ceremonies.

The Herd family parked their trailer, measuring 8 by 35 feet next to four small cottonwood trees below the mesa top and unloaded the milk cans that would hold their water supply. They soon learned that shopping for food required a 160-mile round-trip drive on a narrow dirt road to Holbrook.

They next found the church building: a two-room adobe and rock structure just off the main road, on land traditionally held by the Snake Clan. Inside the building they found an uneven floor, an unpainted altar and pulpit, some rough wooden benches, an upright piano, and a few gas lanterns for evening services. This setup might qualify as "heaven" for a missionary in a remote area of some distant exotic land, but for them it was rustic and 80 miles from anywhere!

Ironically, separatism was forced upon the Herds almost from the start. Although the children were very happy attending the school at Polacca with the Hopi children, after only a few days, an inspector instructed the principal to remove the white children to the Keams Canyon public school, 15 miles away.

Soon afterward, lightning struck the rented house at Shongopovi, a village in which the Herds had been holding services at Second Mesa. To traditional Hopis a lightning strike is evidence of evil within, and the village chief, Kikmongwi, and 12 other elder Hopi representatives met with Brother Herd to discuss several issues. Thirty Hopi women from Shongopovi had been attending services at the time, two of whom were Spirit-filled and had made a full commitment to Christ—something that disturbed the Hopi Council, which feared a disruption of the traditional Hopi Way.

The meeting ended when the Council decided that no more Christian meetings would be held in that village.

But the Lord is wise. Christian meetings continued to be held at First Mesa, and many Second Mesa women found a way to continue fellowship there. Rides were arranged secretly between the Hopi women of Shongopovi and First Mesa believers. "Determination marked their newfound faith," said Mrs. Herd, "and they were able to walk in the Light of Jesus."

A similar disruption of services occurred in Mishongnovi, also of Second Mesa, but this was to have more dire consequences. The Hopi leaders of Mishongnovi threatened the owner of the house in which Christian meetings were held, and the meetings stopped. Fear of a similar retaliation spread to First Mesa, and not only were meetings stopped, but also the space where the Herds had parked their trailer was reclaimed.

In March 1958, the Herds moved their trailer and ministry to Holbrook, where they spent the next 14 years building a church. Beginning in an old rented bank building, they developed a viable church by Easter Sunday, March 29, 1959. It was quite a Resurrection celebration! While pioneering the Holbrook church, the Herds continued to make weekly trips to the Second Mesa villages.

After a year of weekly trips by the Herds, the Hopi leaders decided to forbid any further Christian meetings there at all. "Though not understanding," Mrs. Herd explains, "we left them in His hands and hoped [that] in the future, someone [else] could take them the Good News."[10]

Elizabeth White

The famous Hopi potter Elizabeth White (Polingaysi Qoyawayma), whose family knew the Voths, recorded in her 1964 autobiography that she enjoyed singing songs the missionaries had taught the Hopi children. She sang: "Deso lasmi, deso no" long before she knew what the syllables meant: "Jesus loves me, this I know."[11]

According to Ms. White, Hopi equivalents of those strange syllables translates something like, "The San Juan people are bringing burros," which brought roars of laughter from the Hopi children when they first learned them. She would have been shocked, she said, to have learned that the missionaries thought the children to be unsaved and wicked.

Years later, Ms. White realized that by accepting the new ideas of the white people, she was partly responsible for breaking up the traditional Hopi cultural patterns. She knew that one change changes everything. Christians also need to be reminded that only Jesus is immutable, but people and cultures change. For life to be good and worth living, one must be the child of a perfect Father and know Him. It is the missionary's commission to help others know their perfect Heavenly Father.

Elizabeth White reported that she never was afraid of white people, as some of her family and friends were. During the tension between the friendlies and the hostiles at Oraibi (described earlier), her own father helped missionary Voth build his Mennonite church there. After the Oraibi split, Ms. White's family moved down off the mesa top to the new village of Kykotsmovi (New Oraibi).

About that time, a group of Hopi young people were sent by the government to the Sherman Institute in Riverside, California (which is now one of the most famous Indian boarding high schools in the U.S.) Ms. White went with them and studied there for four years. On one of her visits

Learn the Historical Setting of the People

back home, she met Reverend Frey, who had come with Voth and his wife to study the Hopi language. During this visit, Ms. White converted to Christianity, and she soon was speaking at area churches. Before long, Reverend Frey arranged for her to study at the Bethel Academy was in Kansas. During her three-year Academy course, Frey took her with him on missionary trips to Nebraska and Oklahoma.

From Sunday School teaching, Ms. White went to teach at the Tuba City boarding school, a Bureau of Indian Affairs institution. Again, with Frey's help, she enrolled at the Los Angeles Bible Institute (now Biola University in La Mirada, California). While a student there, she frequently sang as a soloist at the Church of the Open Door. During this time, Elizabeth White was treated as an outsider by her own Hopi people: They accused her of "becoming white," an unkind pun on her English language name.

In her late 20's, Ms. White turned from missionary work to classroom teaching, at first without official certification. She taught english to first-graders at Hotevilla, the village that had been established by Youkeoma and the hostiles. This probably was considered to be a double or even a triple insult to her relatives in Oraibi. After all, her family had moved down from the mesa-top Old Oraibi to New Oraibi; she had become "white" in more ways than one; and now she was teaching in the village that had split earlier from Old Oraibi.

Ms. White reports that the facts were painful to live. Pain is a gift that the Lord sometimes gives to those He has chosen to purify—in order to carry out His eternal plan—and is, in a sense, another form of love.

In 1924, ironically the same year that the U.S. government granted citizenship to native Americans, Ms. White passed her Indian Service test and became a bonafide, certified government employee. During the next 30 years, until her retirement in 1954, Elizabeth White experienced the pain of living in the two worlds of her Hopi traditions and her new Christian beliefs. Ultimately, she would lay all her worries at the feet of the Great Healer and the Great Teacher, Jesus Christ.

One morning in 1982, I sat down in the living room of this world-famous potter, musician, missionary, and teacher and talked with her for a long time. She was unaware of any greatness, fame, or talent. If any of these things might be true, she added, it was to the glory of God that they were. My recollection of Ms. White is one of a dear, sweet, grandmotherly, brilliant woman, at once a beautiful Hopi and a lovely Christian. I mean no irreverence when I say that if the Old Testament had needed one more book with a woman's name, it could have been the Book of Elizabeth.

We Cannot Shake the Dust From Our Sandles

The pastor at the Sunlight Mission, located between First and Second Mesa, has maintained a foothold of sorts as have the pastors at the First Mesa Baptist Church. The Catholic Church is barely present on the Hopi Reservation. A few other denominations have remained marginally effective, but their membership is small and the activity is minimal. A notable number of workers, however, have spent much of their lives ministering to the Hopi people in churches, schools, and other capacities, both on and off the Reservation. The need there continues. Although the Hopi have rigorously resisted the gospel, we cannot afford to "shake the dust from our sandals" and move on. They are our brothers and sisters, and we are responsible for them. We are our brother's keeper.

Learn the Historical Setting of the People

Reassess the Methods

Historically, the Hopi have not been treated well by white people, but God's grace heals many wounds. It is obvious that the average Hopi person considers Christianity as "white man's religion." Sadly, Christians often confuse opposition to Christianity with a rejection of the gospel but they are not the same thing. Often we have failed to recognize that it is our methods—and not the gospel—that is being resisted.

The notion that a person can progress without taking risks is false, not only spiritually but in all other areas. We must remind ourselves that we live in a fallen world and that some measure of loss or damage is unavoidable. We cannot allow evangelistic progress to be hampered by false assumptions that certain closed societies are actually closed to the gospel. The Hopi have the same right to the gospel as anyone else, and the fact that they have tenaciously clung to their traditional ways is not justification for this mission field not being "white unto harvest."

Leaning on our own imperfect understanding is unwise and we dare not fail to evangelize because of an assumption rather than experience. In Jesus' "Parable of the Talents," the cautious servant was more concerned with the potential for loss than with a failure to gain. The possibility of "not doing better was sacrificed on the altar of not doing worse."[12] The story ends with the servant's realizing his worst fears (see Mt. 25:14-30).

It is truly regrettable that our history of missionizing the Hopi has left such an indelible negative impression upon so many contemporary Indian people. Blame for this sorry reputation can be laid primarily upon a fundamental confusion on the part of our early government between "civilizing" the Indian and "Christianizing" the Indian.

During the entire British colonial period, attempts were made to Christianize the Native Americans, actions based upon the governing power's limited understanding of the concept. President George Washington, in his 1791 address to Congress, offered a program for future dealings between the newly created United States and the Indians. (The Indians were not considered to be an integral part of the United States at that time.) The President's program included "experiments" for imparting to the Indians the "blessings of civilization" which, of course, included conversion to Christianity. It was not long before "civilizing," "missionizing," and "educating" became synonymous terms. All these were imposed upon the Hopi, more or less, by force.[13]

Friendship Takes Time

The desert is not pretty, unless you know where its beauty lies. Nor is it friendly, until you've lived there long enough to make it a friend. It is sparse and seemingly barren of grass, water, and trees. The people of this region are not unlike the desert. They are hardy, contented mostly to carve out an existence from the land that is their home. Although the Hopi's past has defined his present life, Jesus Christ has the power to define his future.

The same can be said for the unbeliever next door that appears unresponsive to your Christian testimony. His traditional values and personal lifestyle may be threatened by the gospel. Images of overzealous evangelists might lurk in the recesses of his memory. Whether we are facing the mission field of our back yard or alien nations, we have to ensure that we do not tread on the graveyards of their past with disrespect.

Like the Carruthers, we must be willing to be innovative in our approach; like the Herds, we must be wiling to redefine the "map" of theology; like Elizabeth White, we must be unafraid of painful service; and finally, like Jesus, we must show them the Father's love.

Just as the Father has loved Me, I have also loved you; abide in My love...This is My commandment, that you love one another, just as I have loved you. Greater love has no one than this, that one lay down his life for his friends (John 15:9;12-13).

Chapter 3

Recognize Obvious Biblical Parallels

> *...God made it evident to them. For since the creation of the world His invisible attributes, His eternal power and divine nature, have been clearly seen, being understood through what has been made, so that they are without excuse* (Romans 1:19b-20).

Just as you need to understand their history, you also need to learn and respect the religious culture of the people you are working with—to acknowledge your common ground and proceed in a positive way. Regardless of where you are in the world, God's Word tells us that all creatures have a knowledge of the Creator.

My experience with the Hopi has taught me to embrace the common ground we share with a thankful heart, respect the differences, and trust God to transform the darkness into His Light. The Christian principles we profess are often put to the test when we encounter people who see the Creator differently than we do. An objective scientific mind will recognize obvious parallels between the Hopi oral scriptures and the biblical accounts.

Syncretism

I do not believe in syncretism, which proposes that all religions present different valid ways to find God. The syncretist takes the parts he likes from one religion and combines it with another. (See Chapter 6 for a complete discussion on syncretism.)

The following example used in witnessing to Hopi and other culturally different people not only addresses syncretism, but also attempts to clarify the historical progression which the Hopi people surely must have followed to "leave" a one-God religion and "arrive" at a seemingly many-god religion. The stories of Hopi genesis and migration are now a part of my own experience and after years of prayer and study, the Lord has clarified many issues for me regarding the Hopi and their imperfectly remembered Scriptures.

I responded to one Hopi man's question: "But you have only one God and we have so many different ones." I gave him the following explanation: "We already have talked about Jesus and the Holy Spirit. Although each one is a separate personality, they, along with the Father, are all one God. So when I say, 'God,' you understand that three different personalities may be addressed, separately or collectively? Throughout the Old Testament, the ancient Jews assigned many different names to the various aspects or attributes to the one God Jehovah. The ancient Jews were like the Hopi in this practice."

"You know the Twenty-Third Psalm, 'The Lord is my Shepherd'. Let's say that one day you feel a special need of God's protection, and you call on Him. But instead of calling Him Jehovah Shepherd, you just call Him, Shepherd, and pray, 'Dear Shepherd.' Another time you are sick and you need healing. And rather than calling on Jehovah Doctor

(Rapha), you just call Him, Doctor, and pray, 'Dear Doctor.' Now on a third occasion, you need money. And rather than calling on Jehovah Banker (Jireh), you simply call Him, Banker, and pray, 'Dear Banker.' "

"Now over the years God takes on three names, Shepherd, Doctor, and Banker. Over decades or maybe centuries, not only do these names prevail, but also the mental images that the names suggest replace the original; in your mind you see a shepherd, a doctor, and a banker. In human terms, one God has 'become' three. But the wonder of the one true God is that He is also Jehovah Shamma, God-is-with-us. He will not allow you to forget Him. He placed the truth in you, and this truth remains somewhere in the back of your memory. Just as He told the nation, Israel, through Joshua, when the mantle of leadership passed to him from Moses: 'I will not fail you or forsake you' (Josh. 1:5b). God repeats this promise to the New Testament Church: 'I will never desert you, nor will I ever forsake you' (Heb. 13:5b). He never left the Hopi either! The Hopi stories clearly connect the many Hopi deities—Spider Woman, Maasaw, and others—with the one Creator, whom you call Taiowa. So, you see, there is only one God called by many different names, both in the Scriptures and by the Hopi. And He is the same yesterday, today, and forever."

Anthropology

I do not suggest a cultural connection between Hopi and Jewish practices in the usual anthropological sense. Just because two different cultures do or think the same is not proof on its own of cross-culturalization, cause-effect, or borrowing between the two cultures. I insist that only one Truth exists, just as there is only one God.

Evangelizing the Culturally Different

What I do suggest is that the Hopi have been, from time immemorial, copying the one and only Truth of God. But since the Hopi possess only an oral language, much of the original Truth has been lost or remembered imperfectly. I believe that the Hopi Way is a corrupted and incomplete version of God's Truth.

Therefore the chief goal of an evangelist in a cross-cultural situation is to divide the culture points of contact (beliefs, traditions, ceremonies, foods, clothing, songs, dances, etc.) between culture and scriptural truth. The best way to do this is to study both Scripture and the alien culture very carefully.

The Independent Discovery Theory

I do not subscribe to the independent discovery theory. Among numerous explanations for similarities and identical motifs between biblical and Hopi accounts, anthropologists tend to lean heavily on the idea that, because all humans possess the same thinking mechanism and because humans face a limilted number of different problems and dilemmas, they are likely to hit upon the same or similar solutions at widely different times and places.

While the independent discovery theory is eminently reasonable, the comparison of Hopi and biblical accounts results in a number of astounding similarities and parallels. In some place these accounts are identical.

Oral Literature

The total wisdom of the Hopi Way (somewhat analogous with the Holy Scripture) is oral literature, which includes all myths and traditional stories. Although Hopi wisdom is disseminated through all of life's activities, the chief medium of instruction is the "story." These stories sometimes vary in detail from village to village, storyteller to storyteller, and performance to performance. Although the interpretation of Holy Scripture may vary somewhat from exposition to exposition, one assumes that the modification is likely to be of a lesser degree than Hopi story retelling (even though some Hopi performers possess prodigious memories) because the Bible is a written text.

Although no one has collected all traditional Hopi stories into a single source, I suggest these might contain much (possibly all) of the Old Testament text. In order to communicate clearly, I opt to use the term *story,* because it is more inclusive and less narrowly defined than *myth, legend, parable, proverb, and the like. By story,* I mean "all varieties of narrative, including those just listed."

The Hopi lineage goes beyond retrievable history. We know they are an ancient people, certainly predating the well-studied Anasazi of the twelfth century. Like all other people, they were created by the only God that exists, and "...that which is known about God is evident within them [those He created]; for God made it evident to them" (Rom. 1:19).

The great Christian thinker J.R.R. Tolkien firmly believed that traditional stories or myths (not false or fantastic tales) "originate in God, that they preserve something of God's truth, although often in a distorted form...The Christian story [is] a myth invented by God who [is] real, a God whose dying could transform who[ever] belie[ves] in him."[1]

Tolkien suggests that presenting a myth may be doing God's work. Upon hearing these very words, C.S. Lewis (the century's greatest Christian apologist) was converted to Christianity in a biblical manner: "A mysterious rush of wind came through the trees that [Lewis] felt to be a message from the deity."[2]

Where Does Truth Come From?

As stated in the Introduction, I have used the word *Truth* to represent both "Word" and "Light" as synonyms for the Greek word *Logos*. *Truth* stands for "the complete work of God in the person of Jesus Christ." God's Word declares:

> ...*I* [Jesus] *am the way, and the truth, and the life; no one comes to the Father, but through Me* (John 14:6).
>
> ...*I* [Jesus] *am the light of the world; he who follows Me shall not walk in the darkness, but shall have the light of life* (John 8:12).
>
> *In the beginning was the Word* [Jesus]*, and the Word was with God, and the Word was God. He was in the beginning with God* (John 1:1-2).

Consider that God's Word as we know it (the Bible), has been translated into a number of versions or variant readings within the English language. We can agree that these variations have been made to communicate to a diversity of English speakers who have a multiplicity of experiences. (Updating archaic forms and vocabulary was also a consideration, but not the primary one.)

In the New King James Version, Matthew 24:28 reads "For wherever the carcass is, there the eagles will be gathered together." In the New International Version the same passage uses the phrase, "the vultures will gather." The contemporary English speaker, in general, is aware that vultures devour carcasses, although he probably does not think of eagles performing this activity. For most of us the word *vulture* carries nasty connotations, while the word *eagle*, with its association of "freedom" and "America the beautiful," probably does not. No matter what the genetic connection between the vulture and the eagle may be, the typical image of an eagle is likely to be different from that of a vulture. Yet the fundamental *meaning* of the Matthew passage is the same.

The Bible has been translated for people with widely different experiences. Whether the name *Jesus* is rendered "Jesucristo" in one language and "Jesu" in another is of little significance. What is vital is that the name refers to the same *Person*; "the only begotten Son of God" (see Jn. 3:16).

Language is a system of organizing images. The ancient Jews were familiar with images such as "shepherd," "streets of gold," and the like. However, the Hopi experiences were quite different and they did not possess a written language. Consequently, a Hopi parable could appear *prima facie* to be different from an ancient Jewish one, but the meanings might be identical. Only the images vary to suit the environment.

All Truth is from God, while all lies are the work of the enemy. Consequently, where traditional stories match the biblical account, I believe they are true. At points where they vary, the enemy has had a hand in arranging the error. The prime directive for all believers is to make God's Truth real to unbelievers and to unmask the enemy's lies.

The Sacred and the Ordinary

Story is not an illusion but is both spiritual and practical to the Hopi. The Hopi Way makes no formal distinction between practical and spiritual affairs; the two are intertwined. Westerners are constantly aware of time measurements, whereas the Hopi are aware of mythical timelessness. A Hopi acquaintance once remarked, "Of course Hopi aren't stupid. We know the difference between today, yesterday, and tomorrow, but just don't run our lives by clocks and calendars."

Hopi, of course, recognize a difference between the spiritual and material planes of experience. The two realms presuppose each other, and each is necessary for the other. Hopi people simply experience the spiritual through the profane material forms and rhythms of life (such as birth and death, the seasons, and planting and reaping) in a way that most Westerners do not.

The Hopi people refer to the sacred by two different terms—*a'ni himu* or *hikwsi*—which translate approximately, "very something" or "giver of the breath of life."[3] The people represent this "breath of life" literally by a small fluffy white feather, tied with a piece of cotton yarn. One can see these breath feathers tied to people's hair (particularly right after a sacred ceremony has been performed), attached to brush near springs and wells, or even hanging from a rearview mirror. These breath feathers have been ritually prepared by a holy person in the *kiva* prior to a ceremony (see Chapter 4 for a description of the *kiva*). The *breath feather*, sometimes called a "prayer feather," represents a special blessing.

The Hopi Worldview

Although many names occur in the Hopi creation stories, the Hopi people are not polytheistic (i.e. believe in many gods). Rather, they worship one spiritual substance that manifests itself in different modes. Similiarily, Christians call upon Jehovah God by various names, depending upon the need.

Recognize Obvious Biblical Parallels

The Hopi believe that they were created by a distinctly Hopi deity to dwell upon a specific *promised land* in uniquely Hopi ways. This formulation compares favorably (almost to the point) with the ancient Hebrew concept of a peculiar relationship with their Jehovah God in the Promised Land, separate from other peoples of the earth. Hopi genesis (a number of ancient traditional tales that the Hopi people retell regularly in the various sacred ceremonies today) echoes the biblical Genesis account, and I consider it a variant. "Be sure it is not for nothing that [God] has knit our hearts so closely to time and place—to one friend rather than another and one [land] more than all the land."[4] The Bible records:

> "In the beginning God created the heavens and the earth" (Gen. 1:1). "...The Lord God formed man of dust from the ground, and breathed into his nostrils the breath of life..." (Gen. 2:7). "...The Lord God sent him [Adam] out from the garden of Eden, to cultivate the ground from which he was taken" (Gen. 3:23). "...God blessed Noah and his sons and said to them, 'Be fruitful and multiply, and fill the earth'" (Gen. 9:1). "Now the Lord said to Abram [Abraham], 'Go forth...to the land which I will show you; and I will make you a great nation...'" (Gen. 12:1-2). [God said to Israel through Moses], "I will also redeem you...I will take you for My people, and I will be your God; and you shall know that I am the Lord your God..." (Ex. 6:6b-7a).

The Hopi Genesis

If you were to ask a Hopi person today why he experiences so much tension between the traditional ways of his people and the ways of the contemporary world, he would probably tell you that this is because he is living the last days of the Hopi Fourth World.

The Gap Theory

One fascinating (yet unprovable) correspondence is the Hopi concept of four worlds. According to their scripture, the Hopi people have passed through three worlds, are presently living in the fourth, and are expecting a fifth. More than one Bible scholar, including the late J. Vernon McGee, insist upon the so-called "gap theory." Genesis 1:1, they say, presents the first creation. Something went wrong and God destroyed that creation. Genesis 6:7 is their proof-text: "And the Lord said, I will destroy man whom I have created from the face of the earth; both man, and beast, and the creeping thing, and the fowls of the air; for it repenteth Me that I have made them" (King James Version).

According to the gap theory, Genesis 1:2 is the creation we are presently acquainted with. "And the earth was formless and void, and darkness was over the surface of the deep; and the Spirit of God was moving over the surface of the waters."

The gap theorists insist that God created a cosmos, not a chaos. Isaiah 45:18 (Amplified Version) provides the proof-text for this assertion: "For thus said the Lord Who created the heavens, God Himself Who formed the earth and made it; Who established it and created it not a worthless waste. He formed it to be inhabited—I am the Lord, and there is none else."

Although the gap theory has gone out of fashion, no one to my knowledge has proven it false or untenable. If these theorists are correct, it goes without saying that there may have been other creations prior to that of Genesis 1:2, the one that Adam and Eve inhabited. We know that Adam's world was destroyed. We are certain of two worlds, before and after Noah. Is it not possible that Hopi scripture has

Recognize Obvious Biblical Parallels

managed to preserve more information than Old Testament studies have yet managed to make certain?

However, I only cling to what I am certain of—Romans 1:20 is beyond challenge: "For since the creation of the world His invisible attributes, His eternal power and divine nature, have been clearly seen, being understood through what has been made...."

The First World According to Hopi Scripture

The First World was endless space, or *Tokpela*. Only the Creator, *Taiowa*, existed. Then the Creator created a Son, *Sotuknang*. In Hopi kinship terminology, the Son would be called "Nephew" because Hopi children are under the discipline and guidance of their mother's oldest brother and not their biological father. (I will use the term "Son" for easier identification.) It was the Son who created the earth, substances, and forces.

The Son, in turn, created Spider Woman, the archetypal grandmother *Kookyangwuuti*, who was to remain on the earth of the First World, *Tokpela*. Spider Woman (often called Spider Grandmother) created a pair of twins, *Poqangwhoya* and *Palogawhoya*, by scooping up a handful of dirt, spitting into it, and molding the clay into two figures. She covered the two figures with a cape (or mantle) of white substance and sang the Creation Song over them. These Twins completed the solidification of the earth and tuned it to the Creation Song. Spider Woman then created all the vegetation, birds, and animals. Then Spider Woman created mankind in three phases.

First, she formed four males in the same way she had made the Twins, in the image of the Son. Then, she formed four females in her own image to be their partners. In phase one, the eight forms came to life. In phase two, the breath of life came into them. In the final phase, they faced their Creator: the Son.

Each human couple, male and female, was a different color: yellow, red, white, and black. Spider Woman gave them instructions to demonstrate wisdom, harmony, respect, and love for the Creator at all times. Then she gave each couple a different language, sent them off in four different directions, and admonished them to be happy and multiply.[5]

These are fascinating variations of Genesis 1:1, "...God created the heavens and the earth"; Genesis 1:22, "...Be fruitful and multiply..."; and Genesis 11:7, "...Come, let Us go down and there confuse their language...."

The First People (the prediluviun race) forgot to respect their Creator and lived wickedly. They fought and drew away from each other, forming different races and different languages because they listened to the Talker, *Lavaihoya* ("a mocking bird"). A very handsome one, *Kato'ya*, disguised himself as a snake and led the people even further away from the Creator's ways.

The Bible tells us that satan is a liar and a mocker and can disguise himself as a snake! Genesis 3:4b-5 shows us satan's craftiness: "'You surely shall not die [said satan]...For God knows that in the day you eat from it [the tree of life] your eyes will be opened, and you will be like God, knowing good and evil.'" Verse 13 records: "...And the woman said, 'The serpent deceived me...'."

According to Hopi genesis the Creator decided to destroy the evil First World, except for a faithful remnant: "You are the ones we have chosen" (note the plural "we"). He gave the chosen ones these instructions: "Go to a certain place. Inner wisdom will lead you. You are to follow a certain cloud by day and a certain star by night. Your journey will not end until the cloud stops and the star stops. After many days and nights they arrived at this certain place."

Maasaw, a "guardian spirit," told the Hopi people how to carry out their migration. This holy being gave the people a number of stone tablets that had "written" instructions for proper living.

(This could have been a form of hieroglyphics, or there is possibly a written language that is now lost.)

It was prophesied that *Pahana* or *bahana,* "a light or white-skinned" individual, would come to them one day and "deliver them from their persecutors." *Maasaw* warned the people that if they accepted and followed anyone but *pahana* they would die.

The Son, *Sotuknang*, appeared and told them to follow Him. He led them to an underground place, the *kiva*, where they lived with the Ant People (maybe literal, maybe metaphoric), while the Son (at the Creator's command) destroyed the earth's surface by fire. The chosen people lived safely within the sacred *kiva*. This was the end of the First World.

The Second World

It took a long time for the First World to cool off and a Second World to be created. Finally, *Sotuknang* purified the old world and created a new one. When it was ready, the Son told the people, "Remember your Creator and the laws He gave you," and He ordered them to emerge to the Second World, *Topka*. The people multiplied rapidly and spread out over the earth in all directions.

Soon, however, the people began to quarrel and fight. A few people still respected the laws of the Creator, but the wicked ones just laughed at them. Once again, the remnant went underground to stay with the Ant People, while the Second World froze to solid ice and the whole planet ceased to rotate on its axis. (Some attempt to connect this story motif with the Ice Age, assuming it to be a racial memory.)

The Third World

Eventually, *Sotuknang* ordered the Twins to cause the earth to revolve again and move back into its universal orbit. When the earth was ready for occupancy, *Sotuknang* told the people to emerge into the Third World, *Kuskurza*. During the Third World, the people developed cities and countries. Before long they turned their thoughts to their own plans and forgot the laws of the Creator.

The chief sin of the ancient Hopi was sexual licentiousness (unlike the idolatry of the Jews, although there might conceivably be a connection between the two). This time *Sotuknang's* anger was so great that he decided to destroy the world again. He told Spider Woman to gather up all those who had not been corrupted and to seal them in hollow reeds. She did so, and the Son flooded the earth. After a long time the water receded, leaving the reeds on the top of one of their highest mountains. Spider Woman instructed the remnant of people, telling them that their own spirits would guide them. This was the Fourth World, or *Tuuwaqatsi*.

The Fourth World

Upon reaching the Fourth World, the people were met by the guardian and caretaker of the land, *Maasaw*. At the beginning of this Fourth World, *Maasaw* ordered the people to divide into groups and to migrate to the four corners of the world. "Go and claim the land," He said to them. "But if you turn again to evil ways, I will take the earth from you." And with this, *Maasaw* disappeared.

Biblical Parallels or Coincidence?

I do not believe the Hopi to be as far from the biblical account as some have imagined. Time, oral recountings of the stories (with accompanying elaborations, variations in performance, memory slips, and possible deliberate falsifications), and the lack of a written language can account for almost all variation between the two accounts. The Hopi have had a written language for the past few decades, but some traditionalists still do not recognize it.

I would not *force* the Hopi and biblical Genesis accounts into a perfect parallel structure, nor intend to fabricate the scenarios in order to make the two mesh. However, God's

Recognize Obvious Biblical Parallels

revelation of His Truth has always been incremental: People have not received the same components of the Truth at the same time. Certainly the ancient Jews knew Jehovah God in a way that the Gentiles of the same period could not identify with. God revealed Himself to Moses before Jesus was revealed. Jesus was revealed before the Holy Spirit. I urge you to consider the following:

> The biblical first world was destroyed by water; the Hopi by fire (see Gen. 6-7).

> The Hopi First World people were misled by a mocker, which resulted in a division of races and languages. This echoes the account of Nimrod and the Tower of Babel (see Gen. 10:9-10 and 11:1-4).

> The Hopi deception by a snake, the handsome one, powerfully echoes the temptation by Lucifer (see Gen. 3).

> The motifs of the remnant—the certain cloud and the certain star—surely resonate within the memory of every student of the Old Testament. A pillar of fire described as a "certain star" is not a difficult mental adjustment, particularly when it is coupled with the idea of a pillar of cloud and a certain cloud (see Ex. 13:21-22).

> The Creator created "the Son." Jesus is called "the sun of righteousness" (see Mal. 4:2).

> The Hopi Son destroyed the evil First World by fire at the Creator's command. Jesus the Son is in command during the Great Tribulation when the earth is partly destroyed by fire (see Rev. 8:7).

It is foolish to be dogmatic about that which cannot be proven, yet it is just as foolish to ignore strong identical or near-identical material when we know that biblical accounts are the Truth and that all Truth is from God. Where Hopi accounts agree with biblical accounts, I believe that they are true!

Old Testament students can see similarities between the numerous rebellions of the ancient Jews with their God and the ancient Hopi people with theirs (the progression through the first three worlds). As recorded in Nehemiah 12-13:1, there are also some striking parallels between some contemporary Hopi practices and the ancient Jewish practices:

> The ancient Jews were separated into tribes and clans, just as the Hopi.
>
> The Jewish priests helped to dedicate the wall with thanksgiving, music, and song. The *kachinas* purify themselves before ceremonies, dancing, and singing.
>
> During the dedication of the Jerusalem wall the leaders walked in opposite directions, giving thanks. They used the original instruments of King David. In contemporary *kachina* ceremonies, the dancers turn to each of the four directions and give thanks. They use drums, rattles, bells, gourds, scrapers, and other ritual paraphernalia that has been passed on from generation to generation.
>
> The people brought a daily supply of food for the singers and the priests. Likewise, food-sharing constitutes a vital aspect of Hopi ceremonials, both for the clan priests as well as the general populace.
>
> The Book of Moses was read to the people. Contemporary Hopis tell their stories in cycles, especially at winter solstice ceremonies but at other times as well.

The Hopi have have kept their "holy scriptures" alive by the grace of God, Who loves them as He loves all His creation. To summarize the entire Hopi Way is as insurmountable a task as reducing the Old and New Testaments to a few paragraphs; neither is possible. Nonetheless, an outline of Hopi genesis and a knowledge of the Hopi worldview is vital to anyone attempting missionary efforts among the people because these are wonderful points of contact for the unbeliever.

Living With a Painful Paradox

The contemporary Hopi experience a painful tension between their traditional teachings/practices and the technological/industrialized Western world. The paradox of eternal myth and historical change is faced with sorrow, but the change, itself, is understood as the fulfillment of Hopi Way prophecies.

One prophecy, for instance, declares the dominance of white people, so present circumstances of white domination are considered fulfillment of the prophecy. The people cope with the encroachment of American modernity by deliberately making the decline of their religion sacred.

God's Truth Does Not Change

If, until now, you have interpreted Truth solely from your own religious or denominational perspective, I urge you to give this matter prayerful consideration. Remember, God's Truth does not change. However, the package He presents it in sometimes does, without weakening the biblical account in any way.

For we know in part, and we prophesy in part...For now we see in a mirror dimly, but then face to face; now I know in part, but then I shall know fully just as I also have been fully known (1 Corinthians 13:9,12).

Chapter 4

Learn and Respect the Cultural Context

Only conduct yourselves in a manner worthy of the gospel of Christ; so that whether I come and see you or remain absent, I may hear of you that are standing firm in one spirit, with one mind striving together for the faith of the gospel (Philippians 1:27).

The world grows smaller every day. Overseas products are delivered to our communities with the efficiency of a well-oiled machine. Most countries boast of international food chains and ethnic restaurants. Personal computers bring cultural diversity into the office, classroom, and home with only a few keystrokes. Communities, schools, and churches consist of diverse racial groups. Government agencies and schools employ bilingual men and women to meet the growing demands for foreign languages. Geographical boundaries no longer define cultural limits as they once did.

Ideas of creation, after-life concepts, religious traditions, social customs, apparel, and even food preferences not only identify one culture from another but also open and close doors to the salvation message. Although the unbeliever may appear to reject the gospel message, it is often the cultural context of the message that lies at fault.

Anyone who has read James A. Michener's *Hawaii* cannot forget the early missionaries' experience there, particularly the sad passage delineating the missionary requiring his son to wear long wool underwear in August because "all proper New Englanders put on their long wool underwear in August."[1] This example may seem extreme, but early Spanish missionaries to the indigenous people of Mexico literally burned every single sacred object and piece of sacred writing they could find, assuming in their ignorance that all such items were pagan and satanic. The evangelist who allows his own culture to dictate right and wrong corrupts the love of God and presents a distorted image of the Creator.

Clan Patterns

Since the Hopi emerged into the present Fourth World, they have been divided into clans, each one tracing its ancestry to some clan symbol, ancestor, or mythical clan ancestor collectively referred to as *wu'ya*.

Nearly all clan names come from the names of plants, animals, or supernatural beings.[2] All these phenomena are easily seen in Hopiland today. In order to understand Hopi kinship patterns (a difficult task for an outsider), it is essential to understand clan ancestors.

Kinship System

Contemporary Hopi have a reverent closeness to the phenomena associated with their clan name—Eagle Clan members feel an association with the eagle, Corn Clan

Learn and Respect the Cultural Context

members with corn, and so on. This clan system, even today, is the dominant dimension of socialization for the Hopi people.[3] Each individual belongs simultaneously to several clans by virtue of the fact that the kinship system allows a Hopi to relate to several aspects of the world.

Elizabeth White, *Polingaysi Qoyawayma,* has a unique corn design pottery that is both beautiful and internationally admired. My Hopi friend who took me to see her knew that he was (in some way) related to Mrs. White but had never met her before. The two of them talked for mere seconds in Hopi before howling with laughter. Mrs. White was his granddaughter! This was particularly startling because at the time she was in her 80's and my Hopi friend was barely 50.

Don Talayesva's published autobiography *Sun Chief* is a classic of Hopi literature. He was born of the Sun Clan and received his name from his ceremonial father after initiation into the *Wuwutsim* Society, one of the four main men's fraternities. *Talayesva* means "sitting tassel" and refers to the top of greasewood and bamboo; his ceremonial father belonged to both the Greasewood and Bamboo clans. Talayesva is linked to five different groups of clans, each of which consists of three or more clans. As a result, Talayesva is affiliated with 22 clans.[4]

As Louis Hieb (a scholar in Hopi studies) discovered, a Hopi does not say, "I am the same flesh and blood as my parents," but instead says, "I am the liquid substance of my father [ancestors]."[5] Hopi social structure recognizes no dichotomy between the spiritual and the natural, so a conception of the clan as a timeless and permanent group is basic to the understanding of relationships.

Because of these interconnections, a Hopi experiences a certain transcendence over a strictly human status. In addition, the intertwining of the spiritual and material dimensions serves to identify and relate all Hopi to each other and their world.

In light of the Hopi's interrelatedness through clan as well as bloodlines, the evangelist must be very sensitive to the native sense of obligation to kin and his understanding of roles of leadership and subordination. For instance, food-sharing with certain relatives is a traditional requirement. Hopi males are responsible for several female relatives outside the Western concept of a nuclear family. Also, a Hopi would consider it outrageous for a bloodline mother to chastise her own son, because guiding and punishing the Hopi boys is the role of the oldest maternal uncle. In fact, all Hopi (as is common in many other alien cultures) are related to each other more directly than in the Christian view.

Do Your Homework!

You must be aware that to engage an individual member of a culture may be paramount to engaging a whole network of people whose traditional obligations to each other (and also avoidances) are binding within their culture. Learn and respect the cultural context of the people with whom you work. Sadly, many evangelistic opportunities have been lost or greatly delayed because a well-meaning evangelist did not do his or her homework.

Definitions Change From Culture to Culture

The average westerner usually regards *myth* as "an intangible tale that holds little, if any, substance." This definition is in direct opposition to truth. However, myth is not an illusion to the Hopi people, but reality both spiritual and

Learn and Respect the Cultural Context

practical. (Academic folklorists have, in fact, applied the term *myth* to what probably ought to be *story*.)

For example, Hopi tradition holds that Spider Woman, (Kookyangwuuti), taught the people how to weave in ancient times. She was the first weaver, and her techniques and patterns have stood the test of timelessness. Consequently, when a contemporary Hopi weaves, the act is not the result of his own efforts, alone, but rather a manifestation of the creative process of Spider Woman. This is not an example of spiritism: "Spider Woman" is a name and image assigned to one particular attribute of God, i.e. "Jehovah Jireh" (see discussion on page 79-80).

Westerners are constantly aware of time, and in fact, we are slaves to it, while the Hopi are aware of timelessness—a never-ending process of being or an eternal unfolding.

Knowing this cultural aspect can become a point of contact for the evangelist. God is the same yesterday, today, and forever; yet, He is constantly and gradually revealing his mighty Truth (Heb. 3:8).

All That Is Called Demonic Is Not

Not all evangelists have (or are expected to have) a college degree in Bible studies, anthropology, mythology, or the like. Many well-meaning Christians launch into evangelical ministries with limited frames of reference and occasionally fall into the trap of assuming that anything that shocks their personal worldview or cultural expectations must be demonic.

For example, an evangelist only familiar with Western musical concepts is apt to misinterpret the droning repetitious singing style of the Hopi or the high-pitched, seemingly frenzied singing style of the Apache and Navajo

Indians. Similarly, the drums, rattles, and scrapers of various sorts may appear to be unseemly before God.

I have heard well-meaning Christians describe Native American musicians (and those of other alien cultures) as "demon-possessed." I even encountered a sad example of this while Indians performed their version of "The Pledge to the American Flag."

Psalm 150 describes a variety of instruments and their music. It tells us to praise God with loud cymbals, stringed instruments, timbrel, harps, lyres, and trumpets. We are told to play skillfully with a loud noise unto the Lord. Does this sound at all like the refined symphonic instruments of Western concert halls or solemn religious hymns?

C.S. Lewis writes of the ancient Jews as being more of a "feeling" people than an analytical people in matters of sacred worship.[6] I submit that the Hopi are more feeling than analytical in this regard. For them (as with the Jews) music, dance, and festivity are not separated from worship: In a sense, all of life is a piece of worship.

Consequently, the sound of drums, rattles, and dancing are virtually synonymous with religious experience or (more accurately) the presence of the supernatural. Proof of this phenomena was demonstrated to me while I was attending a church service on the Hopi Reservation in the 1980s. The handful of participating Hopi were recent converts to Christianity.

Don't Throw It All Away

During the singing of a particularly exuberant worship song, I asked, "Why don't you incorporate your traditional drums and rattles?" I thought that this would be aesthetically quite pleasing. My question stopped the show!

Learn and Respect the Cultural Context

An elderly Hopi, with horror on her face, gave me this forceful explanation, "When we play the drum, *that* spirit comes. When we shake the rattle, *that* spirit comes. This is the house of Jesus," she said. "Those spirits are not welcome here."

After a quick silent prayer for guidance, I pointed out that many people consider rock music guitars and loud drums inappropriate for God and worship, yet many Christian musicians have demonstrated that guitars and drums are merely a means of making music—even sacred music of a profound nature. She agreed but appeared unconvinced about the rattles and drums.

I continued to explain, "Either evil spirits are present in them or they are not. Do you believe that the Holy Spirit is dwelling within you?"

"Oh yes," she replied.

"Do you think that the Holy Spirit recognizes evil spirits?" I asked.

"Sure!" she responded.

"Well, then," I said. "All we have to do is speak to the rattle and drum and we will know. The Holy Spirit will help us to discern the truth."

Since she thought this was a good idea, I urged her to speak to the instruments with me and to trust the Holy Spirit within us to tell us the truth. We did so, but the instruments did not say a word.

I continued the discussion further, pointing out that her Hopi religion had sustained her people for hundreds of years. I urged her not to throw it all away. We are prone at times to throw out the baby with the bath water. "God has been watching your people since the moment He created them," I went on, "with an eye toward bringing you and your people to His Son and holy perfection. Because of this, all things in the Hopi religion are not evil. In fact, much of it is God's revealed Truth."

God always honors the hearts of those who seek His Truth. Finally, I allowed that the rattles and drums are beautiful to the ear. When they are played unto the Lord, they are holy and precious to the Creator.

My Personal Experience

I have personally attended at least a dozen or more Hopi ceremonies. This includes the *Home Dance* (at the end of which the *kachinas* return to their "home" in the San Francisco Peaks to remain for one half of the year), and the universally famous Snake Dance.

I have watched the *kachinas* arrive in the villages early in the morning, and I have participated in sprinkling sacred cornmeal on the priests, who are intercessors between the people and the Creator and vice-versa. I have requested blessings from the *kachinas* who have bestowed gifts both upon me, my grandson, and friends.

I have talked at length and in detail with participants in the various ceremonies and learned about the ritual preparations of the cornmeal, water, tobacco, masks, costumes, songs, dances, and much more. I have witnessed an attitude of holiness, awe, and respect for the Creator and His creation.

On each occasion, I have prayed to Jehovah God and He was present. I sensed His Holy Spirit in the drums, the rattles, the songs, the dances, the beautiful masks, the costumes, the grinding gourds and scrapers, the sacred clowns, the

Learn and Respect the Cultural Context

Hopi houses, the sky, the earth, and the people themselves. After testing the spirits, I sensed no satanic involvement.

I published a short novel several years ago, where I described my view of a recent Hopi Dance. I was a born-again, Spirit-filled Christian at the time, and was in awe of what I experienced:

> The dancing of the Kachinas was exciting, absurd, beautiful, grotesque, elevating, sacred. The non-human heads and intense movements [of the dancers] was awe-inspiring. The long and repetitious songs [they appeared so at the time] seemed monotonous, but filled with an intensity of feeling and sensibility to which I was foreign [completely so at the time]. I tried to think of these things as a Hopi might, but I could only observe them objectively...I was young then and failed to grasp much [of what I saw and heard]. [While I watched], my mind went back to [my] early Christian exposure and understanding of [another] experience which also seemed to be grotesque and uplifting at the same time. I [had] watched the reverence with which people handled the little [plastic] cups of wine that were supposed to be the blood of Christ, after having seen the ladies of the church in the kitchen pour Welch's grape juice....[7]

Kachina Homage

Various groups of people came together from migrations to live in unity. Therefore it is now virtually impossible to trace the source of some of these traditions. Matters concerning the *kachinas* constitute a doctrine with various interpretations.

The Hopi do not consider the *kachinas* to be deities. The Western culture does not have an exact parallel to the *kachina*, but if one were to pressed to find a complementary idea, he might imagine a guardian angel or guardian spirit sent by God. *Kachinas* are "helpers, assistants bridging the gap between the spirit realm and the natural realm." They are not worshiped in any way.

Plants, animals, heat, and the power of lightning are called *kachinas*. Even humans upon death become *kachinas*, sometimes called "ancestor spirits" who move within this supernatural world. All *kachinas* (frequently called "cloud people"—indicating their spiritual nature) are rain-bringing agents whose residence is in the San Francisco Peaks (near Flagstaff, Arizona).

According to Hopi scripture, the *kachinas* live for six months in the villages and six months in the mountains. According to myth, the *kachinas* used to live in the villages all the time, but when the people started acting bad, the *kachinas* decided to remain in the villages only half of the year.

Barton Wright, Scientific Director of the Museum of Man (San Diego) and a knowledgeable man on Hopi ritual, gives a clear and succinct account of the *kachina* cult. "Corn is the Mother of the Hopi" and without corn there is no food. Hopiland receives scant rainfall and "capricious weather is the norm." Consequently, the Hopi feel a need to obtain supernatural assistance to ensure the growing of corn. Long ago, this need was formalized into a complete cycle of rituals and ceremonies.[8]

Don Talayesva, the late Hopi Sun Chief, says that the "ceremonies are extremely complicated...usually performed for the express purpose of ensuring rain...."[9] The Hopi believe that God and the universe are totally reliable and will assist man, if approached properly. The world is a duality of the natural and supernatural. As in Plato's doctrine, the natural world has forms of mass and solidity, while the unseen realm has spiritual shapes. The natural world is a mirror of the supernatural. Hopi assign important forces (such as wind and water), living form also. These

Learn and Respect the Cultural Context

forces, if approached properly through sacred ritual, will assist humans. In Hopi thought, there are many such beings.

Prophets or Prognosticator?

Contemporary Hopi tell me their prayers only work upon Hopiland. Whether a Hopi ceremony brings rain to Los Angeles or Phoenix, I do not know, but I have never attended a Hopi ceremony upon Hopiland that did not bring rain before its conclusion.

Some have posited the theory that Hopi people are especially good weather prognosticators and so only perform their rituals just before a rainfall. This seems untenable because many ceremonies require several days of preparation—a success rate of weather forecasting far superior to anything we have seen among so-called scientific meteorologists. The supernatural element (it seems to me) cannot be dismissed. After all, the prophets of old were able to bring rain (see 1 Sam. 12:18-19). I find no reason to doubt that the Hopi also communicate with God in a similar fashion.

Kachina Ceremonies

During *kachina* ceremonies, the *kachina* dancers are personified by masked and costumed men who prepare for these rituals for many days, sometimes by fasting and prayer. While Christians think of giving up food during a fast, Hopis abstain from sexual contact and the ingestion of salt. Most of the actual ceremonies and some *kachina* dances take place in the underground *Kiva*. Most dances, however, are held in the open village plazas.

The ceremonial cycle, and the number and type of *kachinas* (more than 380), constitute a complexity that goes beyond the purpose of this book. *Kachinas* exist in three forms: the spiritual, the personified dancer, and the intricately carved dolls that the Hopi use primarily to teach the

Evangelizing the Culturally Different

children. (See Bibliography for Barton Wright, Frank Waters, and John D. Loftin. They give reliable and detailed accounts of the *kachina*.)

At the beginning of this century, according to Don Talayesva (Sun Chief), virtually every Hopi above the age for initiation (7 to 11 years) belonged to the *Kachina* Society.[10] By his or her initiation, a Hopi child has gained the right to enter the Land of the Dead after death. During this initiation the novice learns that the ancestors were Cloud People who returned to Hopiland as *kachina* ancestor spirits.

If an unschooled non-Christian were to reflect upon certain Christian worship practices, he might draw disparate conclusions as to their possible holiness. The Christian church traffics in much representational art: statues, pictures, and icons of various kinds.

Christian dramatic performances sometimes move us deeply. Christians are fully aware that a man costumed as Jesus is not Jesus, or even the Spirit of Jesus. We do not confuse statues with what they represent. We might pray while kneeling before a statue, but not to it. Catholics ask the Holy Mother Mary and other saints to intercede for them. They take the Scriptural admonitions to pray for the saints as well as to petition the saints (see Rom. 8:27, Eph. 6:18, and elsewhere).

The masked and costumed *kachina* dancer is a personified ancestor spirit. When the typical Christian missionary encounters 100 masked *kachinas*, dancing and singing rhythmically to drums and rattles, it may be foreign, fascinating, and a bit unnerving. Hopi music is utterly alien to Euro-American ears, and Hopi dancing is unlike any social or classical form. The media has associated Hopi music and

Learn and Respect the Cultural Context

dance with savagery and barbarism, and this association has tragic consequences for the Hopi.

Unfortunately, missionaries have seen or heard about the *kachinas* and—in their limited Judeo-Christian upbringing—draw facile conclusions, perceiving them as "satanic beings."

Preparation Is the Key

Have you ever noticed that a young boy in our society loves his first baseball game but hates his first opera? There is a very good reason for this: The boy's father has told him every detail about baseball, demonstrated the techniques involved, and played the game with the boy. The boy has been prepared. He has seen the game in his dreams.

On the other hand, the boy's mother, assuming that her son will respond to opera in emotional ways similar to hers, thrusts him into the experience unprepared. He finds himself watching people in odd costumes and screaming loudly in a foreign language to loud music coming from noisy instruments. He is overwhelmed, thoroughly disappointed, and possibly a little frightened.

The key to understanding (or at least appreciating) any new experience is preparation. The missionary facing unfamiliar ceremonies—like the young boy facing the opera—must be prepared to make sense of what he sees. In addition, one must be certain that she is prepared properly and not influenced by fabrications and stereotypes.

One native American poet—Juanita Bell—has a wonderful poem called "Indian Children Speak." In the poem, a young white woman goes to college to learn how to teach Indian children. Her teachers give her the official scoop about Indian children: they are non-verbal, excessively shy, and unloving. When she arrives to teach the Indian children, she discovers that her students are not only very verbal but also wonderfully poetic in their use of language. They follow the rules of appropriate Indian behavior by not looking others in the eye, and they love to hold her hand and talk with her about their feelings.

Animal Imagery

Stories about "Brother Turtle," "Brother Deer," and "Brother Coyote" abound in Hopi oral scripture. Terms like "Brother," "Sister," "Grandmother," and such, are relational to a degree through clan lineage. A person, however, is only ostensibly related to an animal; he is related to the *character* of the turtle, deer, or coyote rather than to the animal per se. He does not mourn the death of an animal with the same kind—the same amount—of grief as a human. They are quite separate.

In ancient times, however, according to Hopi oral scripture, animals did walk and talk as humans. If this seems curious, we must remember that the serpent in the garden also spoke and apparently walked upright before God put a curse upon him (see Gen. 3:14).

Jehovah God is referred to 6,828 times in the Bible as "I Am." Not long after His initial revelation to Abraham, however, certain words were added to the name, "Jehovah." We find "Jehovah Jireh," Provider (Gen. 22:14); "Jehovah Shalom," Peace (Judg. 6:24); Shepherd (Ps. 23:1); "Jehovah Maccadeshem"(Ps. 23:5); Sanctifier (Ex. 31:13); and "Jehovah Shammah," With You (Ezek. 48:35). These descriptive names, along with many others, represent characteristics or attributes of God.

Learn and Respect the Cultural Context

The names were cultural. The ancient Jews were acquainted with such things as shepherds. The Hopi, in a similar fashion, are familiar with turtles, deer, and coyotes. Is it not eminent good sense for a desert people to associate God's slow, deliberate steadfastness with the characteristics of a turtle?

Concepts Remain Constant

I do not suggest that there is a direct parallel between the ancient Jewish concept of "Jehovah Jireh" and the Hopi concept of "My Brother the Deer" (both are providers). However, the similarity of characteristics, those that Christians attribute to "Jehovah Jirah" and those that Hopi attribute to "Brother Deer" is striking.

Perhaps if the Hopi had a written language, there would never have been a need for anthropomorphic parallels. But we must remind ourselves that the Hopi culture has relied on the oral transmission of concepts. Words and labels change over the years, but concepts tend to remain remarkably constant.

Animal Imagery Is Not Animism

Although some scholars have described Hopi animal imagery as a pure case of what anthropologists call "animism," the worship of animal spirits, I am inclined against this based on my many Hopi friends and acquaintances. Animal imagery and animal relationships are, instead, metaphoric references to the various characteristics and attributes of the Creator.

Functionally, this is much the same as the Christian's use of the image of a dove to represent the Holy Spirit. The dove is a representation: an icon, not deity. Most contemporary Hopi seem to deal with this phenomenon in this fashion.

Christians should have no difficulty with the animal imagery of the Hopi culture, since Judaism and Christianity are filled with animal imagery. The "fiery serpent" that the Lord commanded Moses to provide healing is one example (see Num. 21:8-9).

Interpretations Do Vary

It is true that objective discussions regarding cultural relationships and ceremonies might vary. Natives (of any culture) may understand the same phenomena differently. Christians also misperceive biblical doctrines from time to time. The evangelist should simply deal with it in a calm, loving manner and bring the gospel to light. The possibility of such an encounter is precisely why the evangelist must learn and respect the ideas and icons that resonate in the minds and hearts of the people with whom he or she is working. If you plant a good seed of righteousness, you will reap a crop of God's love.

Hopi Ceremony

The entire course of the Hopi "Road of Life" unfolds every year in an annual cycle of religious ceremonies, a series of parables that dramatize the universal laws of life. In a culture lacking a written language, these ceremonies parallel many dramatized Bible stories.

The Old Testament gives detailed description of the feasts and celebrations that God commanded Israel to keep (see Ex. 23:14-15; Lev. 23,25; and Num. 28,29). The commemoration of these festivals is still an integral part of Jewish worship. Christians recognize their prophetic significance

Learn and Respect the Cultural Context

in the life, ministry, death, and Second Coming of Jesus Christ.

During the Middle Ages, the Roman church performed many such plays to commemorate events and teach Bible truths to an essentially non-reading peasant class, especially at Christmas, Easter, and other holy days. Today, it is essential for the missionary to familiarize himself or herself with the elementary aspects of religious ceremonies on their particular mission ground.

The nine Hopi ceremonies or "mystery" plays are not unlike the Medieval mystery and miracle plays of the European Middle Ages and are performed yearly. With a modicum of study and preparation on the part of the onlooker, these ceremonies should not seem strange, bizarre, savage, or barbarian.

The songs and dances form recognizable patterns, although musically the songs are often polyrhythmic with many sudden shifts of accent. Although they are sometimes quite complex in their structures, the novice need not concern himself or herself with this aspect. The onlooker is not likely to see anything more unusual than a deer horn, an eagle feather, a turtle-shell rattle, a twig of spruce, an ear of corn, or daubs of mineral paint. The cornstalk, stones, and other elements of nature are significant, but these are only symbols of the spirit that gave them form. These forms are mere manifestations of the one supreme Creator.

The Kiva

The *kiva* is an underground chamber where preparations are made and rituals are held—a sacred place also used by members of that fraternal society for meetings and tasks such as weaving. Each fraternal society has its own *kiva* sunk in the plaza at the center of the village, the *kisoni*, where public dances are given at the conclusion of the ceremonies. The central part of the *kiva* protrudes four or five feet above the surface of the ground. Inside, the floor of the eastern half is raised slightly above the level of the western half. During initiation rites, the novices occupy the raised level and the priests remain on the lower level.

Scholars have tried to make much over the fact that the Christian church is built above ground, the thrusting steeple is a phallic symbol of its patriarchal history, and the Hopi *kiva* is below ground, a symbol of Mother Earth's womb, expressing a matriarchal past. Whatever this difference might mean (possibly nothing), the missionary must realize that the Hopi possess great reverence for the earth. During the winter months, when Mother Earth is pregnant and waiting for the birth of spring, traditional Hopi will not cut or dig into the soil, or even walk roughly upon the earth.

The center of the *kiva* is on the altar level and just below the roof opening, with a sunken fire pit for the New Fire Ceremony during *Wuwuchim*. Beside it sits a small hole in the floor called the *sipapuni* (the navel path), which represents the umbilical cord leading from Mother Earth. The altar is set in the floor's center, and a seating ledge runs across the west wall. Directly opposite the ladder there is a house that contains the *kachina* masks when not being worn by the men impersonating the spirits. The ladder represents the reed that people climbed during the Emergence.

The Pahos (Prayer Sticks)

The preparation of the *pahos* (non-Hopi call these "prayer sticks" or "prayer feathers") is a prime requisite of all ceremonies conducted in the *kiva*. The *paho* is made from any kind of feather, but eagle feathers are normally used.

The male-and-female *paho* consists of two red willow sticks about eight inches long. Beautiful and symbolic, both may be painted blue, although sometimes the male is painted black. The female stick has a facet cut in the upper end, which is painted brown. Tied to the base of the sticks and binding them together is a small sack made of a corn husk folded to a point—the *noosioqa* (nourishment), which is symbolic of the spiritual body. Cornmeal (representing the physical body), a pinch of pollen (power of fertility), and a drop of honey (the creator's love) are inside the sack. Both sticks are tied together with a cotton string, and an eagle feather (representing the breath of life) is tied to the end of the string. In Hopi stories this is often referred to as a "breath feather." It reminds me of Genesis 2:7; 22-24:

> *Then the Lord God formed man of dust from the ground, and breathed into his nostrils the breath of life...And the Lord God fashioned into a woman the rib which He had taken from the man...And they shall become one flesh.*

Cornmeal Is Holy

Hopi ceremony cannot be conducted without the use of cornmeal, which is a substance used in much the same manner as Catholic priests use holy water: Objects and people are sanctified by the sprinkling of sacred cornmeal upon them. Sacred paths are marked by lines of cornmeal for *kachinas* approaching the village, and all roads and paths are blocked to living creatures. Dancing *kachinas* are sprinkled with cornmeal.

Baskets and woven plaques of cornmeal are common offerings during all rituals. Ears of colored corn (called "Corn

Mothers") designate the six directions (north, south, east, west, up, and down) and are stacked at the base of the altar. Seven ears of corn are tied to the staff of the corn clan kachina, called *Aholi*. Another is tied to the "Law of Laws," called *Mongko*. The number seven, of course, resonates in the mind of all Christians, as does the "Law of Moses" that was read at the end of long ceremonies by the ancient Jews.

For an in-depth view of Hopi ceremonialism, one should read Edmund Nequatewa's *Truth of the Hopi* or Frank Water's *Book of the Hopi*.

The *Wuwuchim*

The *Wuwuchim* (germination) ceremony denotes supplication by the participants to the Creator by recreating the first dawn of creation (including all forms of life on earth: plant, animal, and humankind).

The ceremony takes place during November (*Kelmuya*). On the first day, participants gather the materials for making the *pahos*. On the second day, the Crier Chief publicly announces the beginning of *Wuwuchim* from a housetop. The entire ceremony lasts 16 days, with preparation period of eight days, culminating with a public dance in the plaza on the last day. (It generally is recognized that ceremonies originally in the village of Oraibi—and now Hotevilla—are the purest forms. Those on First Mesa are supposedly the most corrupted because they have been contaminated by Tewa and Navajo influences.)

After the public announcement by the Crier Chief, participants enter the *kiva* for preparations and purification of themselves. On the ninth day, the priests enter their *kiva* for a second eight-day period. It is said that only the Two Horn

Learn and Respect the Cultural Context

Society possesses the complete and original concept of creation and that this is the most important society participating in the *Wuwuchim*.

I have witnessed the fact that there is a spirit of holiness during the period of ceremony preparation. I have remained outside the *kiva* to observe and listen to the audible ceremony preparations. Hopi are no more perfect than Christians and drink alcohol just as non-Hopi do. One hot summer day I witnessed a priest quietly castigate a dancer who had been drinking. The priest hastily remove him from the plaza.

On the fifteenth day, a member of the One Horn Society in full ceremonial costume emerges from the *kiva* and closes each road by drawing four sacred cornmeal lines across it. (Four main roads or trails lead into Oraibi from the four directions.) He seals the village from any evil power that might come. By prayer and this physical act, he, like the Christian, binds the enemy.

Not until morning, when the ceremony is over, are the roads opened again by a One Horn priest who cuts the cornmeal lines with his chief's stick or *mongko*. Only one trail is left open, through which the holy beings are invited to enter and inhabit the village. The spirits emerge from their home at the beginning of this trail, an invisible opening somewhere in the San Francisco Peaks. This act compares favorably with the Christian's invitation for the Holy Spirit to inhabit those places where the enemy attempts to gain strongholds—our cities, our homes, and our rooms.

The *Astotokya*

The chief ceremony is so sacred that it is rarely discussed: the Washing of the Hair, or the *Astotokya*. This ceremony is held every four years, when there are initiations into one or all of the four *kiva* societies.

All Hopi children are initiated into either the *Kachina* or *Powamu* Societies before the age of adolescence. *Wuwuchim* initiates are young male adults who are inducted into a higher stage of spiritual training. They are seated on the raised floor at the eastern end of the *kiva*. Only after the ceremony is completed, and they have been ritually confirmed to the pure pattern of creation, are they allowed to come out. (The Washing of the Hair brings to mind the careful purification and anointing rites of the ancient Jews for novices about to enter the temple.)

As the initiates are given full instruction in their role as a mature Hopi, all the men representing the spirits of the past and other worlds (fully robed but unmasked) file around the three sides of the altar level.

While this is happening, a lone white-robed figure enters the *kiva* and announces, "I am the beginning and the end." He is *Nutungktatoka*, the first and the last. He leaves the *kiva* as quietly as He came in. Can this white-robed figure be any other than a representation of the biblical great "I Am"?

Then a yell sounds, and all participants inside the *kiva* scramble to climb out through the ladder in the roof. As they exit the *kiva* top, they are drenched with buckets of water, symbolically washing away all their wickedness. In essence, they are baptized.

At the public dance on the last day of the ceremony, the priests file out through the narrow causeways of the village to sing and dance in the little open plaza. All the people living in the village actively participate by offering prayers,

Learn and Respect the Cultural Context

blessing the dancers with sacred cornmeal, or bringing food to share. Visitors and outsiders participate by observing.

Pray for Fruitful Encounters

Regardless of where we take the Good News of Jesus Christ, we are going to encounter cultural differences and tribal rituals. This might be as simple as participating in the personal dining etiquette of another family or as complicated as visiting a Native American Indian ceremony. How we respond to and work with the existing culture will make the difference. If we have eyes to see the common ground we share, our encounter will be fruitful and the gospel light will shine from our lives.

Arise, shine; for your light has come, and the glory of the Lord has risen upon you. For behold, darkness will cover the earth, and deep darkness the peoples; but the Lord will rise upon you, and His glory will appear on you. And nations will come to your light, and kings to the brightness of your rising (Isaiah 60:1-3).

Chapter 5

Kingdom Culture Guidelines

For wisdom will enter your heart, and knowledge will be pleasant to your soul; discretion will guard you, understanding will watch over you... (Proverbs 2:10-11).

As God-sent evangelists we proclaim a Kingdom Culture, but we must realize that the Kingdom Culture allows a great deal of diversity. God's creation is wonderfully varied, yet each of us is terribly limited in our knowledge of the whole.

We can rely on the fact that His Word is a lamp unto our feet (see Ps. 119:105). His Word will help us to distinguish between cultural differences that must be respected and scriptural issues essential to salvation.

Second Timothy two addresses the soldier in active service, and the evangelist is a soldier. Verse 14 admonishes him "not to wrangle about words, which is useless, and leads to the ruin of the hearers," but to study and learn so that he may handle the *Word of Truth* accurately and effectively (see 2 Tim. 2:14). In an almost mind-boggling complex world—one in which my politeness is your offense and your politeness is my offense—many interpersonal and cross-cultural skills and tools must be acquired in order to successfully deal with people different from us.

Soon after the Los Angeles riots of 1992, a serious cultural conflict came to light. Korean merchants in the area and their African American patrons had been experiencing tension for a long time. People finally realized that in Korean society (and in Asian societies, in general) it is disrespectful to physically touch other people. (Remember that Americans consider a slap on the back a friendly gesture.) Korean merchants, to show respect for their patrons, were placing change on the counter for the patrons to pick up. Americans, ignorant of the cultural expectation, thought, "They think they're too good to hand the change to me!" The Korean politeness became an offense, and vice-versa.

Cultural offenses often occur. Those interacting with other cultures simply do not understand the impact of their words and actions. Kingdom Culture representatives have a responsibility to share the gospel with God's love (see 1 Cor. 13:1-13).

Some areas that have caused concern in the past are attire; male/female roles; methods of worship (costumes, music, and dancing); food, drink, and lodging restrictions; respect for privacy; interaction and avoidance of physical contact; misinterpretation of courtesy; and a lack of respect for deep-rooted beliefs.

The Proper Attire

A colleague of mine accepted a mission to South Africa in 1995. He held prayer meetings in the open, usually under a tree, in wretchedly hot and humid weather. The native men arrived in two-piece dark suits with long-sleeved shirts and neckties, and the women wore Western-style dresses.

Kingdom Culture Guidelines

I observed the same kind of Western attire in the hot humid climate of Montego Bay, Jamaica. This amazed me because Jamaica is a land in which men typically wear nothing above the waist and women wear loose-fitting garments. Most everyone goes barefoot.

It goes without saying that some missionaries (either explicitly or implicitly) *taught* these native people about the "proper" Christian attire. Here in the West, feelings about Christian apparel are a mixture of regional tradition, family upbringing, denominational guidelines, and personal taste. Some American religious spokespersons disallow make-up, jewelry, or pants for women, while prescribing the typical suit and tie for men. Others draw the line only with exposing of too much skin at either end of the body. Nearly all seem to scrutinize women more than men.

The evangelist working among culturally different people must resolve two issues regarding proper attire. He must rely on more than just feeling. First, he needs to know what the Bible has to say. Second, he needs to learn the values of the culture.

The second chapter of James teaches against showing partiality to the well-dressed. While this passage specifically speaks about showing favoritism toward the wealthy, its message may be applied to personal prejudices (see Jas. 2:1-12).

The issue of attire must be resolved, even to the point of partial or full nudity. One must realize that in numerous cultures, bare breasts and even uncovered genitals are fully acceptable. Climate and manufacturing resources are prime factors that often determine how much of the body is covered.

The Genesis account of Adam and Eve makes it clear that both man and woman were naked prior to the Fall. It was the presence of God in the Garden, after their sin, that caused them to feel ashamed of their nakedness. Embarrassment over nakedness—not nakedness itself—was the result of the Fall. It was God's holiness that made Adam and Eve feel the need to cover themselves (see Gen. 3).

I suggest that it is not the evangelist's job to *cover* the nakedness of those to whom he is witnessing. Instead, it is his job to bring the gospel. Native people in Africa, New Guinea, the Amazons, and other regions have reported that people who once accepted nudity began to cover themselves as a result of the gospel. A culture that lives under the influence and guidelines of the gospel is truly a *Kingdom Culture*.

As for yourself, always dress modestly and be apprised of local expectations. Almost universally (with some notable exceptions) women are expected to cover themselves modestly. In many regions shorts are considered to be offensive. Often bare shoulders are not welcome, and on occasion the head is expected to be covered.

It is also important to note that the attire of one people is often offensive to another living in the same or contiguous region. On a recent trip to Jerusalem, I inadvertently offended one Jewish man by wearing traditional Arab headgear near the famous Western Wall (the Wailing Wall). I had worn the large scarf (or *keffiah*) because it shaded me so well from the blazing sun. I apologized, removed the scarf, and put on one of the Jewish *yarmulkas* provided for tourists. Had I been more sensitive to the Jewish-Arab political and religious tensions, I would not have caused this man the stress that I did. More extensive coverings for females, such as the veil, are expected in many parts of the Moslem world.

Kingdom Culture Guidelines

Male/Female Roles

Anthropologist Margaret Mead discovered a native New Guinea group that demonstrated a full reversal of western male/female role expectations. Females did all the hard work, while males spent most of their time dancing and wearing flowers.[1] Missionaries are encountering stress in the Middle East among the Arabs because of the careful separation of men and women. It is very difficult for the evangelists to talk to members of the opposite sex, so witnessing must take place on a one-to-one basis. Of course, proselytizing is strictly forbidden by Islamic law.

Methods of Worship

Cuetzalan, Puebla, in southern Mexico, is a rural village of indigenous people high in the mountains above the city of Puebla. Their Christian worship services incorporate numerous native elements. The statue of Our Lady of Guadeloupe is ubiquitous through Mexico, but the people of Cuetzalan also incorporate drums, rattles, whistles, the burning of copal incense, dance, and ancient costumes. Elaborate and beautiful dances are performed outside in the plaza before the church service begins. Inside, the church is adorned with a mixture of Christian and native motifs and icons.

I mean no disrespect when I suggest that their celebrations might topple the dignity of many traditional Christians. Yet the power of the gospel has done its work: These people have a profound love and devotion to Jesus Christ. The rest can be likened to "family traditions" such as Santa Claus at Christmas. The beautiful celebrations I witnessed at Cuetzalan remind me of the magnificent celebrations that King David wrote about in the Book of Psalms.

God's ways are higher than our ways. His thoughts are not our thoughts. God's creation is almost infinite in its variety. This is part of His glory (see Is. 55:8-9).

Food, Drink, and Lodging

I suggest that you always accept food and drink if offered to you. In general, non-Euro-Western people—especially tribal groups—are offended if you refuse food or drink. These groups may view such a refusal as a rejection of themselves. On the plus side, they are understanding if you do not like the food or drink. They are fully aware if what they offer is very spicy, bitter, or sour, and they understand the meaning of "acquired taste."

This may be a way to test your sincerity. Regardless, you will all have a good laugh if you taste something that is difficult for you to swallow. Very spicy foods are the norm in hot regions—the result of living without refrigeration.

Similarly, if offered lodging for a night or longer, you should take it. Opening a home to you is a sign of acceptance. An old adage says that you never know a person until you see him at home. To the extent that you can, do as the natives do. When you are in their homes, you can be sure that they will listen to your presentation of the gospel by both the life you demonstrate and your words—if only out of politeness.

Respect Their Privacy

Be aware that some groups do have *secrets*—things exclusively for their own people. The Hopi are a prime example of this. Always be gracious if you are disallowed to participate in or attend certain traditional rituals or ceremonies.

Virtually all people have special or even sacred events that attend what anthropologists call the "rites of passage," those moments of birth, death, puberty, engagement, and marriage. We all have our traditions, although they may not be secret. If you are barred from something, do not be offended. Secret rituals might include such things as the preparation of foods, ritual costumes, music, or prayers. Not everyone is invited to actually witness a circumcision, for example. Your respect for privacy will increase their esteem for you and possibly draw them closer to the Light you shine.

Also, you may be prevented from going to traditional sacred places: altars, caves, shrines, and wells. The Hopi for example, have sacred wells that are ceremonially cleansed cyclically. Also, many of their religious ceremonies, for native people only, are closed to outsiders.

Avoid Physical Contact

Avoid touching children, especially infants, unless you are certain that the native people are pleased to have you do so. Some groups have taboos against non-family members touching children. Rarely is this a health issue; it is usually a fear of spells or curses being cast upon the child.

In the city of Safed, Israel, a center of ancient mystical religion, you will see that nearly all doors to buildings are painted blue. This color is believed to ward off the so-called "evil-eye." These people are afraid for strangers to look directly into their children's eyes or to touch them, so they wear amulets around their necks to counter just such a possibility. Amulets and icons of safety are common throughout the world, such as Jamaica, where a fear of Voodoo practice exists.

Do Not Misinterpret Courtesy for Agreement

For when Gentiles who do not have the Law do instinctively the things of the Law, these, not having the Law, are a law to themselves, in that they show the work of the Law written in their hearts, their conscience bearing witness, and their thoughts alternately accusing or else defending them, on the day when, according to my gospel [Paul is speaking], *God will judge the secrets of men through Christ Jesus* (Romans 2:14-16).

The long Hopi's tradition of non-confrontation has engendered the people with a politeness and opaqueness of emotional demonstration that is enigmatic to the average Westerner. Just because a Hopi listens with polite courtesy to a Christian attempting to explain a point of theology and then responds with a, "Yes, I see," it does not follow that he or she is in agreement. Likely, the response merely intends to communicate, "Yes, I understand what you are saying."

An elderly Hopi friend once shed some light on a typical Hopi attitude regarding spiritual/religious matters. My friend's two sons were mimicking and making fun of some Christian worshipers they had observed in a church service. Their father chastised them rather severely with these words: "Never fail to respect anyone's worship of his god. His ways may be different from our own, but we must respect all people and their beliefs. This is the Hopi Way."

What a wonderful and loving attitude! God's grace has maintained an openness among the Hopi and this very attitude leaves the road open for sharing the gospel.

When talking casually with the average Hopi, it is easy to assume that he is no different from you. The Hopi is conversant in contemporary issues in much the same way as you are, and to the same degree. Except for the very old people, he probably attended public school and has read the same books that you did. He is likely to know as much as you do about sports, politics, and movies. Probably nothing in the conversation will cause the slightest discomfort or confusion, and you are likely to conclude that the two of you are of the same mind.

However, if you were to touch certain topics (religion or sacred ceremonies), you might observe a slight change in facial muscles and a slight shift of eye position. A certain evasiveness might ensue. These are cues that the Hopi person's view of eternal matters is based on such an entirely different set of assumptions that he deems real communication with you on such matters as too difficult—perhaps impossible. Furthermore, to the Hopi, the very secretness of certain sacred matters is part of their power. Exactly what goes on during the preparation of certain sacred ceremonies, for example, is rarely shared with an outsider. To do so might negate the ceremony's effectiveness.

Some differences are fundamental and instructive. The *kachina* dolls are more likely than not to strike you as fascinating examples of Hopi folk art: lovely, beautifully crafted, and entirely bizarre. To the Hopi, these dolls are religious figures of profound significance. The Hopi associations with the *kachina* dolls are somewhat analogous to your own emotional and spiritual associations with artistic representations of the Last Supper or the Crucifixion.

Do Not Treat Witchcraft as Nonsense

During the fall of 1982, while I was living on the Western Navajo Reservation and teaching at the local public secondary school, I formed a friendship with a 30-year-old Hopi. He was living at Second Mesa on the Hopi Reservation with his common-law wife and her family. He would come to Tuba City (about 50 miles from his house) every other weekend to visit friends. He usually slept at my mobile home apartment, so we had opportunity to talk. I often shared the gospel with J. P. and he listened politely, but he appeared to be neither impressed nor moved by it. To him, it was "white man's religion."

On the Monday before Christmas J. P. was sitting on my front doorstep when I came home from work in the late afternoon. Appearing tense and jittery, he apologized for showing up at an unexpected time and asked if he might stay until after Christmas. Since members of my own family were unable to get away from their jobs long enough for a trip to northern Arizona, I was glad to have someone to talk to during my two-week Christmas vacation. I silently thanked the Lord and heartily welcomed J. P. to stay.

After dinner, he seemed somewhat calmer and started to explain his unexpected appearance. He knew that I was concerned, but also that I had learned enough about Hopi ways never to ask direct questions about another person's behavior.

He informed me that the witches back in his village had been "drumming and singing" in preparation for a "sacred" ceremony for days. This scared him and he had to leave. Recently, in a moment of financial desperation, he had sold some of his ceremonial equipment that had been passed down for generations from father to son, and he was afraid that someone "had it in for" him.

Because of my knowledge of Hopi witchcraft, I knew exactly what he meant and did not question him about the matter. I told him that I would pray, instead. He seemed to be pleased by both my silence and my offer to pray.

I related to him an incident concerning another Hopi friend who was walking with me across his village one morning. He had leaned over toward me and whispered, "Here comes _____. If he speaks, be polite, but don't look him directly in the eye. He's a witch." Later that same day, this same friend told me where the Witch Society held its ceremonies. He said, "It's just like a regular ceremony, but everything is upside-down and backwards. You never know when witches are around because they can turn themselves into animals."

J. P. concurred with everything my other friend had said, and I believe he was pleased that I respected his beliefs. The missionary always must be mindful of the fact that the Spirit of God is the teacher; his part is to tell the Good News. J. P. visited me often while I lived in Tuba City, and ultimately, I was able to lead him in the sinner's prayer as he accepted Christ as his Savior. He continues to walk in what he calls "The Jesus Way" today.

Without going into a lengthy treatise on Hopi witchcraft, I'll just say that the practice and unquestioning belief in witchcraft is alive and thriving among them. For a more in-depth understanding of Hopi witchcraft, I recommend reading "Hano Wuhti," in my 1986 publication, *The Hopi Way: Tales of a Changing Culture*.[2] "Hano Wuhti" is an account from an elderly Hopi woman. Only the English translation appears in the book because my Hopi friend who translated it believed the Hopi text to be too powerful and dangerous to see printed in the original Hopi language.

I should publically state that J. P. was not the storyteller or informant for that book. Stories are considered sacred, and the Hopi people prefer to keep their sacred materials secret. Those few who do share with an outsider do so only after having developed a trusting friendship. Even so, they maintain a feeling of ambivalence if materials are shared merely out of friendship or for a scholarly purpose. This tendency to keep knowledge of sacred matters secret is a longstanding tradition among the Hopi but an enigma to Christians, who feel strong obligation to share the gospel or any other idea engendering better, happier, and more successful lives.

The Christian who wants to share the gospel with a Hopi must not treat witchcraft as superstitious nonsense. It is real, according to the Bible. Ephesians 6:12 says, "For our struggle is not against flesh and blood, but against the rulers, against the powers, against the world forces of this [the devil's] darkness, against the spiritual forces of wickedness in the heavenly places." The name of "witchcraft" is given to the evil dealings between humans and the enemy.

The Christian can rejoice at yet another point of contact for sharing the Scriptures. Second Chronicles chapter 33 relates the story of King Manasseh, who practiced witchcraft and sorcery. As a result, the Lord caused him to be captured, bound with thongs through his nose, and taken to Babylon. In the king's distress, he humbled himself before the Lord and God delivered him from his captors. Victory and deliverance are always possible with God! We see another example in Acts 13, where the narrator reports Paul's encounter with a sorcerer.

Without any doubt, the Hopi function with an entirely different set of assumptions regarding the spiritual realm than Christians do. There are historical reasons for this schism. Archaeologists, anthropologists, linguistics, and other social scientists have gathered abundant evidence to indicate that all Native Americans are, in fact, Asians.

According to Harold E. Driver, no serious anthropologist doubts this fact. What we now call "Indians" migrated to the New World across the Bering Strait at a time when it was a solid land mass, somewhere between 10,000 to 40,000 B.C. Physically, they "resemble Asians more closely than any other major physical type in the Old World...."[3] Their resemblance is closest to the marginal Mongolians of Indonesia, west central Asia, and Tibet. This Asian population, at one time, covered most of Asia, north and east of India.[4] It does not take a trained eye to note the resemblance between an old Hopi, Eskimo, and Tibetan.

Although Hopi stories do not support the theory of a great Bering Strait migration, no doubt exists in the field of science. But Hopi religion does not line up point-for-point with any of the major Eastern religions: Hinduism, Buddhism, Shintoism, or Taoism. It is essential for Christians to know that Hopi's spiritual assumptions are not Judeo-Christian. They share more similarities with Eastern than Western thought. We may need to remind ourselves (not withstanding) that the Word of God is universal. Christ died for *all* mankind.

> *...He humbled Himself by becoming obedient to the point of death, even death on a cross. Therefore also God highly exalted Him, and bestowed on Him the name which is above every name, that at the name of Jesus every knee should bow, of those who are in heaven, and on earth, and under the earth, and that every tongue should confess that Jesus Christ is Lord, to the glory of God the Father* (Philippians 2:8-11).

Chapter 6

Beware of the Leaven of Exotic Religions

Finally, be strong in the Lord, and in the strength of His might. Put on the full armor of God, that you may be able to stand firm against the schemes of the devil. For our struggle is not against flesh and blood...take up the full armor of God, that you may be able to resist in the evil day, and having done everything, to stand firm. Stand firm therefore, having girded your loins with truth, and having put on the breastplate of righteousness, and having shod your feet with the preparation of the gospel of peace; in addition to all, taking up the shield of faith with which you will be able to extinguish all the flaming missiles of the evil one. And take the helmet of salvation, and the sword of the Spirit, which is the word of God (Ephesians 6:10-17).

Many religious systems and ceremonies are aesthetically attractive, but you must keep your biblical bearings. Always be aware that the enemy will never miss an opportunity to divert you. You will leave yourself vulnerable to deception unless you put on the whole armor of God daily.

Many evangelists and missionaries unwittingly are pulled into a false system of ideas. You must know the difference between biblical doctrine and religious traditions, because some traditions parallel biblical accounts and others do not. Much of the Hopi worldview exists at the human level. The traditions are quite lovely and touching, but they are not biblical and are therefore destructive. Regardless of the mission field, it is imperative that the evangelist know the difference.

The Kingdom Culture evangelist draws this line with God's Word. Our doctrine must be sound. We must have sure a faith that does not waiver, despite objections and questions that are raised. Although we *do* grow tired, and *do* grow weary, He is sufficient for all our needs.

A Discussion of Syncretism

Syncretism is very appealing to the evangelist confronted with opposing viewpoints about God, because it posits that all religions (Christianity, Hinduism, Buddhism, Islam, and others) are very nearly the same. God is pictured on a mountaintop, while all religious systems of thought send men and women up the mountain on various trails from various points. There is a Christian trail, a Buddhist trail, and so forth, and all reach God. All religions of the world are merely variants of the same archetypal struggle to reach God.

This differs from acknowledging parallel stories (such as the Hopi) with sound biblical doctrine (see Chapter 3). Remember, biblical concepts do not change. For example, God is still the Creator, He sent His Son, and man has been redeemed from his fallen state. Imagery may vary from culture to culture, but the truth remains eternal.

A sincere syncretist believes that differing beliefs and concepts can be combined to reach a compromise. He often will challenge the Christian believer to provide rational responses based on man's wisdom. Once man's wisdom is employed, streams of thought easily are channeled into one wide river of human rationale.

Arm Yourself With God's Word

When a Christian believer is faced with a sincere syncretist, he may be challenged to give a rational response—one without reference to biblical writing, which the syncretist may or may not have read but is likely to reject. The Christian believer must respond firmly with God's Word.

God is man's Creator. Man did not create himself, nor did he evolve into something from nothing. The created creature cannot cure his own physical, social, and spiritual diseases. Man must look beyond himself—beyond his own rational mind—to have hope.

Stand Your Ground

As God's representative, you will be challenged. Unbelievers from every locale (family, neighborhood, and other cultures) invariably ask the same questions. These questions can be stepping stones to a dangerous compromise, but those who are armed with the Word of God will be able to respond with wisdom.

What about the people who cannot read, those who have no written Bible?

...that which is known about God is evident within them [all people]; for God made it evident to them. For since the creation of the world His invisible attributes, His eternal power and divine nature, have been clearly seen, being

understood through what has been made, so that they [all people] *are without excuse* (Romans 1:19-20).

My experience around the world has shown me repeatedly that although individuals cannot read or have not heard the gospel, they do have a knowledge of the Creator. It may not be encapsulated in our language or even in biblical imagery, but God has spoken to them through creation. It is up to Christians to build upon this basic understanding.

If God is a good and loving God, how can He condemn anyone to hell and everlasting torment?

> *...the present heavens and earth by His word are being reserved for fire, kept for the day of judgment and destruction of ungodly men...The Lord is not slow about His promise, as some count slowness, but is patient toward you, not wishing for any to perish but for all to come to repentance. But the day of the Lord* [final destruction] *will come like a thief, in which the heavens will pass away with a roar and the elements will be destroyed with intense heat, and the earth and its works will be burned up* (2 Peter 3:7-10).

A person's rejection of Christ alone sends him to hell, not the love of God. The Creator's love for His creation utterly defies adequate description, and we do not or cannot grasp the enormity of what happened in the Garden at the Fall. The Garden was a perfect environment, yet Adam had free will and chose to defy God. As a result, all of us live in a fallen world. All of creation is fallen. Not only are material things polluted, but also every single component of existence is polluted. Viruses, germs, and disease have corrupted health. Pettiness, jealousy, and hatred have tainted our love for one another.

Why did God allow Adam to live?

The response is simple: "Love." God has an awesome love for His creation. Adam's sin broke God's heart. Imagine, if you can, God's voice upon entering the Garden to spend time with His first-born, only to find him missing. "Adam, where are you?" (See Gen. 3:9).

I once took my three year-old grandson to the market. I love that child and love being with him. As I was filling a bag with fruit, I suddenly became aware that my boy was not within eye-shot. I called, "Mijo, where are you?" No answer. My heart began to pound: I live in a city where children disappear. I hurried from aisle to aisle, looking and calling. I rushed back to the spot where I had first missed him. By now, I had lost all reserve; tears were pouring down my face. I was in awful fear and pain. "Mijo," I yelled at the top of my voice, "where are you?" I found him hiding behind a display. I picked him up in my arms, still crying, and said, "I love you. I don't ever want to lose you."

Adam broke his relationship with his Father in defiance and God cried, "Adam, where are you?" God's love for His children is awesome: He punished Adam and put him out of the Garden, but He still loved him.

God made covenants with Noah, Abraham, Moses, and David (see Gen. 2:16,17; 9:1-17;15:18; Ex. 19:5; and Ps. 89:3,24,28.) but men failed to keep all of them. We ignored the prophets and even killed them. God, in His wisdom, made a New Covenant in Jesus Christ to restore fellowship with us (see Heb. 9:11-23). Now, it is up to us.

If God is a good God, why is there so much suffering?

Suffering, seen from the human perspective, seems such a pointless cruelty. As stated above, we live in a fallen world, one in which all elements of nature are corrupted. Not only its physical elements, but also its spiritual and intellectual aspects are corrupted.

However, Christ was born, suffered, died, and rose again in order for us to be restored to the right, pure, and desired fellowship with the Father. Because of these events, Jesus can say: "In the world you [will] have [suffering and] tribulation, but take courage; *I have overcome the world*" (see Jn. 16:33b).

"How long do I have to suffer?"

Suffering is not a mystery but is clearly explained in Scripture: "...suffering produces perseverance; perseverance, character; and character, hope. And hope does not disappoint..." (Rom. 5:3-5 NIV). We know that every tree (believer) that bears fruit (good deeds and obedience to God's Word) will be pruned (allowed to suffer) by the Gardener (God) from observation, we know that pruning is only seasonal, and that its purpose is to bring about improved and increased production. Suffering is *seasonal* and not relentless (see John 15).

Watchman Nee phrased it perfectly when he said, "There is no spiritual growth without adversity" (another word for suffering).[1] The Bible says that our suffering is "for a little while" (see 1 Pet. 5:10).

Just how much suffering and for how long very much depends on how quickly one learns the lesson at hand and the momenteousness of the lesson. Remember how long Abraham waited for his "approved" son Isaac (see Gen. 21:1-7)?

St. Paul, who suffered greatly during his life, was able to say, "For I consider that the sufferings of the present time are not worthy to be compared with the glory that is to be revealed to us" (Rom. 8:18). And joy of joys, Christ comforts us in all our suffering (see 2 Cor. 1:4). Finally, we are told that if we suffer with Him, we shall reign with Him (see 2 Tim. 2:12).

Do Not Compromise Doctrine for Leaven

Although the Kingdom Culture evangelist must be open-hearted and open-minded enough to understand the impact of historical events, recognize biblical parallels, and respect cultural differences, he must never leave sound biblical foundations. The word *compromise* must not be a part of his vocabulary, regardless of the asthetic or rational appeal.

In Chapter 2, I discussed the Mormon missionizing of the Hopi people. Many Americans are aware of the Mormon ideals of family and family-centered activity, as well as a general propensity for "taking care of their own." These values are both beautiful and Christian, yet there are serious conflicts in the Mormon doctrine regarding salvation. Similar examples could be cited in other well-known American cults, and too many Christians compromise doctrine for leaven.

Clothed in the full armor of God and armed with the Bible, you will be able to distinguish between God's truth and the deceptive wiles of the evil one. Skeptical questions will not persuade you to compromise the integrity of the salvation message:

> *All Scripture is inspired by God and profitable for teaching, for reproof, for correction, for training in righteousness; that the man of God may be adequate, equipped for every good work...Preach the word; be ready in season and out of season; reprove, rebuke, exhort, with great patience and instruction...be sober in all things, endure hardship, do the work of an evangelist, fulfill your ministry* (2 Timothy 3:16-17;4:2,5).

Chapter 7

Know Your Rightful Power in Christ

...arise, cross this Jordan, you and all this people, to the land which I am giving to them, to the sons of Israel. Every place on which the sole of your foot treads, I have given it to you, just as I spoke to Moses (Joshua 1:2-3).

Much of the world today is in transition, just on the edge of the Promised Land. In a sense, we are commissioned by no less than Jehovah God Himself to act as Joshua and Caleb did: to lead the way in. As the weight of present problems and the uncertainty of the future presses in on us, "biblical Christianity offers a whole Gospel for the whole person, which, in turn, advances the hope of permanent change."[1]

There is an agent, however, who is constantly at work against the gospel. He does not want to see a Kingdom Culture established in your family, your neighborhood, or the mission field.

Be Aware of the Enemy

You may, in fact, be called upon to deal with the spiritual forces of wickedness in high places (see Eph. 6:12).

Western New Age marketeers have clothed ancient occult practices with contemporary advertising and consumer appeal. Unsuspecting victims have fallen prey to religious philosophies with demonic roots.

Some nations of the world are well-known for demonic activity. Voodoo is widespread in Haiti, witchcraft runs rampant in Hopiland, and demonic possession is common in Sri Lanka.

It is essential for the evangelist to believe that he can deal with the powers of darkness. If he does not, he must either prepare himself or stay away from it. Anyone who has not put on the whole armor of God will be fearful and ineffective.

Knowing God's Word is not the same thing as believing God's Word. For many years I quoted the Word from my mind instead of my heart. In Mark 9:22-23, some people brought a demon-possessed boy to Jesus for healing. They had doubts when they said to Jesus, "If you can help us...."

Jesus replied, "All things are possible to him who *believes*." I have learned through personal experience that the evangelist who believes God will be victorious.

Where Did the Enemy Come From?

The Bible tells us very specifically how the enemy got to be what he is and what he does for a living on a daily basis. The Scriptures tell us that he is already defeated and why we must go on contending with such an adversary. Isaiah 14 describes the rebellion that went on in Heaven long ago. The handsome angel, Lucifer, tried to lift himself up above God and said, "I will raise my throne above the stars of God...I will make myself like the Most High" (Is. 14:13b-14b).

Jesus, with the Father from the beginning, watched satan's expulsion from Heaven. In Luke 10:18, Jesus tells His disciples, "I was watching Satan fall from heaven like lightning." Not only was satan cast out of Heaven, but one-third of the angels who joined the rebellion also fell. Their doom was instantly sealed: "...Depart from Me, accursed ones, into the eternal fire which has been prepared for the devil and his angels" (Mt. 25:41).

As a consequence, satan and his fallen angels now control the earth. These constitute the ruling "prince of darkness," the "principalities," and the "powers" mentioned by Paul in Ephesians 6:12. In fact, the whole world is under the control of the evil one (see 1 Jn. 5:19).

Even though satan is defeated, we must contend with him for a little while longer. He and his army of imps have been defeated, not completely disarmed. Disarming them is a continuous battle for Christians, yet we have the power and their defeat is certain. The fate of the foe has already been set.

The evangelist must be prepared to deal with the *powers of darkness*—real or only imagined. If an evil spirit only is imagined (as in the event of the new convert in Chapter 4), deal seriously, calmly, and lovingly with the issue. If, on the other hand, demonic activity is actual, remember your power in God!

You can speak to the weather, to a spirit of doubt, or a spirit of obstruction in the name of Jesus, and *in faith*, it will be removed (see Mt. 17:20)! Never forget this promise from God. In cross-cultural situations, where so many circumstances are unknown to the evangelist, she must always remain in prayer contact with the Almighty. Plant good seeds of righteousness to reap a crop of love (see Hos. 10:12).

Put On the Full Armor of God

Ephesians 6 describes the Christian's military gear and weapons. We are to put on the belt of truth, the breastplate of righteousness, the footgear of readiness, and the helmet of salvation. Fully dressed, we are to take up the shield of faith and the sword of the spirit. We also are to pray in the Spirit. God's Word assures us that these pieces of armor and these weapons have divine power to demolish.

According to Mark 9:28-29, prayer and fasting are required to successfully cast out some evil spirits. The evangelist must be in constant communication with the Father. She must be able to fast and pray for anointed power.

Remember that it is God, not us, who actually binds the enemy or casts out the demons. The archangel Michael disputed with the enemy, but he acknowledged the Lord's authority to rebuke him (see Jude 9).

I believe that it is our faith—not the unbeliever—that activates the healing power of God in the Name of Jesus. Mark 2:1-4 is interesting evidence of this. The friends removed the roof and lowered the paralytic to Jesus. When Jesus saw *their faith*, He said to the cripple, "My son, your sins are forgiven."

Warfare in Hopiland

A Hopiland witch is someone who has opened a door to the enemy, who allows satan to destroy anything and everything that God loves. Assuming that satan is an unwanted guest and that the witch wants to get rid of him, the evangelist must be able to follow the biblical pattern.

> Do not work in secret! Invite Christian saints, native elders, and recent converts to join you. Explain everything you say and do. Read the Bible verses aloud to them. Recall the words of Psalm 16:8b "Because He is at my right hand, I will not be shaken."

First John 4:4 will encourage everyone also: "…greater is He Who is in you than he who is in the world."

Begin with strong fervent prayer and ask the Lord for guidance and power (see Eph. 6:19).

Invite the Lord to come in. In Revelation 3:20 the Lord says, "Behold, I stand at the door and knock; if any one hears My voice and opens the door, *I will come in to him*…." Do you think that satan will remain in the Presence of Jesus? Leading a Hopi or any other culturally different individual to Christ need not require a salvation prayer essentially different from one you would share with your next-door-neighbor. However, I always feel led of the Holy Spirit to include a few more statements, because he or she is less likely to know some of the things that Westerners tend to take for granted due to education and cultivation. The salvation prayer that I typically share resembles this:

Heavenly Father, I confess that in ignorance of your plan for my life I have been and remain a sinner. I repent of my sins and ask You to forgive me. I know that your Son Jesus died on the Cross for me. Thank You, Jesus, for dying for me. I accept You as my Savior and Lord. From this moment on, I want to live to please You, Father. There are many things I still do not fully understand and some things I do not understand at all, but I trust You, and believe in my heart that You will guide me in everything I do. I believe and trust that You will always answer me when I call on You. In the name of Jesus, Amen.

Call upon God to manifest His mighty power. Establish the Kingdom of Light. Declare that every knee shall bow and every tongue shall confess that Jesus Christ is Lord (see Phil. 2:10-11). This includes the enemy!

Appropriating the power of God's Word through united prayer is the way to destroy satan's dominions. Such prayer transforms nations lives and nations!

Do Not Seek the Spectacular

The subject of spiritual warfare often implies the demonstration of unusual or shocking manifestations. These might or might not take place. The evangelist, however, never should seek the spectacular. The power of God often comes with quiet force. The light simply expels the darkness.

Sometimes we don't even recognize a miracle until after the fact. Mark 8 shows that the disciples failed to grasp the full impact of the miracle where Jesus had fed the multitude with only seven loaves of bread.

Dispel the Darkness Daily

Shine the Light of Christ in your daily round of duties, regardless of what you are doing.:

> ...*walk in a manner worthy of the Lord, to please Him in all respects, bearing fruit in every good work and increasing in the knowledge of God; strengthened with all power, according to His glorious might, for the attaining of all steadfastness and patience; joyously giving thanks to the Father, who has qualified us to share in the inheritance of the saints in light. For He delivered us from the domain of darkness, and transferred us to the kingdom of His beloved Son, in whom we have redemption, the forgiveness of sins* (Colossians 1:10-14).

Chapter 8

Trust the Spirit of Truth

Jesus Christ is the same yesterday and today, yes and forever (Hebrews 13:8).

For now we see in a mirror dimly, but then [when the Perfect One comes] *face to face; now I know in part, but then I shall know fully just as I also have been fully known* (1 Corinthians 13:12).

Evangelizing the culturally different forces one to examine and re-examine his perception of God's Truth. Each time he faces an inter-cultural exchange, the issue surfaces and the question must be asked, "Does this communicate God's Truth or does it distort the God's eternal Truth?" The Kingdom Culture does not depend upon our own worldview. Rather, it is is defined by God's worldview, and we must trust the Holy Spirit to lead us into all Truth.

And I will ask the Father, and He will give you another Helper, that He may be with you forever; that is the Spirit of truth, whom the world cannot receive, because it does not behold Him or know Him, but you know Him because He abides with you, and will be in you (John 14:16-17).

The writer of the Gospel of John tells us that, "In the beginning was the Word...and the Word was God." John goes on to say that God's Truth has existed since the beginning of time. He sent John the Baptist some 2,000 years ago to be a "witness of the light." Then He sent Jesus so that "every man could be enlightened" (see Jn. 1:1-14).

Jesus cast nuggets of God's truth in the form of parables, so that only those who truly sought their meaning would be able to discern them. The truth was heard by many who were unable to grasp it. However, the Scriptures are very clear on the point that anyone who sincerely hungers for and seeks the truth will find it. The key phrase here is, "at the proper time."

And the disciples came and said to Him, "Why do you speak in parables?" And He answered and said to them, "To you it has been granted to know the mysteries of the kingdom of heaven, but to them it has not been granted. For whoever has [the desire to know the truth], *to him shall more be given, and he shall have an abundance; but whoever does not have* [the desire to know], *even what he has shall be taken away from him"* (Matthew 13:10-12).

Three ideas are implicit for a progressive or incremental revelation of the Truth over a long period of time.

God's Truth has always existed.

Portions or specific aspects of His Truth have been revealed to some people and not to others.

He continues to reveal His Truth gradually or incrementally.

David Did Not Know About Jesus

Psalm 110:1 says, "The Lord says to my Lord: 'Sit at My right hand...'." From this psalm about Jesus, it is easy to conclude that David (the author of the poem) could not possibly have known Jesus as we know Jesus. However, he *knew more than he knew.* Throughout history and prehistory, many men have *known more than they knew.*

The Jews Did Not Know About Heaven

C.S. Lewis posits this in *Reflections on the Psalms*. In summary, he says that it seems curious that the ancient Jews of the Psalms knew nothing, apparently, of Heaven.[1] In most parts of the Old Testament, it seems clear that little or no belief in the future existed. The good and the bad went to Sheol. "In Sheol who will give Thee thanks?" says Psalm 6:5. Perhaps God was teaching the nation, Israel, to rely on Him alone, and its knowledge of a Heaven at that time might have impeded in some way the learning of this lesson. Although David could not have known Jesus as we do today, clearly the idea of a future Savior of some sort was with the people of David's time.

Unbelievers Have Received Divine Truth

Not only has God revealed portions of His Truth throughout history to His chosen people, but also He has revealed it to others. Pharaoh Akhenaten (Amenhotep IV) wrote the "Hymn of the Sun," circa the fourteenth century B.C. Akhenaten tore Egypt apart by rejecting his father's polytheism in favor of worshiping a single god. If we believe that God is behind every event (and every Christian is *compelled* to believe this), then God revealed the idea of one God to Akhenaten. And surely no Christian has any difficulty presuming that traditions descending from the Akhenaten pharaoh could have been the very instruments that God used to make Himself known to Moses. No evidence exists to prove this, but the chief point is that a portion of God's Truth was revealed to a pagan, one outside—in both time and location—His chosen nation.[2]

In the eighth century, Homer (author of the *Illiad*) wrote that the "souls" of the men killed in battle went to Hades, but that a drink of sacrificial blood would restore their "ghosts" to rationality. This is one of the most striking anticipations of the Truth. Plato in the fourth century B.C. developed an entire doctrine of immortality of the soul,[3] while first-century pagan Roman poet-prophet Virgil, not long before the birth of Christ, started a poem: "The great procession of the ages begins anew. Now the Virgin returns, the reign of Saturn [corresponding somewhat to the age of innocence and peace in the Garden of Eden] returns, and the new child is sent down from heaven." Virgil, like the earlier pagans entrusted with portions of God's truth, could not possibly have known about the upcoming birth of the Christ Child.[4]

Scholars can cite numerous other stories or myths that predate the revealed truth of Jesus Christ. So when skeptics complain that the story of creation in Genesis and other accounts evolved from earlier stories (pagan and mythical), they are not refuting anything at all.

The term *evolve* is greatly misleading. Stories do not reproduce their species like animals: They are retold by people. Each storyteller either repeats exactly what he heard, or he changes it. It follows then that at every step he adds something of himself to the story.

When a story is retold that might have had no religious significance at first, and it finally achieves the Truth of the Creator, I believe the storytellers have been guided by God. This is the way that a story merely about nature—the sort of myth found in almost all cultures—has been raised above itself by God for His purpose.[5]

His Truth continues to be revealed today through the Scriptures, the gifts of the Holy Spirit, and in other ways to those God has chosen for His purpose. It will be revealed to anyone who truly seeks the Truth.

Preparing for the Bridegroom

A voice is calling, "Clear the way for the Lord in the wilderness; make smooth in the desert a highway for our God. Let every valley be lifted up, and every mountain and hill be made low; and let the rough ground become a plain, and the rugged terrain a broad valley; then the glory of the Lord will be revealed, and all flesh will see it together; for the mouth of the Lord has spoken" (see Is. 40:3-5).

God's Word proclaims that the Lord God is calling all His children to Himself and that we are nearing the end of history. The Bridegroom is coming, and He is calling all nations! Each of us is born in, rooted in, and grows out of God's bosom, and He will never stop calling us until the last syllable of recorded time. Ezekiel 18:23 records God asking, "Do I have any pleasure in the death of the wicked?"

In Revelation, Jesus still is pleading at the opening of the seventh seal, just before all hell is let loose upon the earth. "When He [Jesus now as King] opened the seventh seal, there was silence in heaven for about half an hour" (see Rev. 8:1 NIV). Most biblical commentators refer to this space of time as the lull before the storm of destruction of the earth, near the end of the Great Tribulation.

I do not believe that this half hour of silence is wasted time. I believe that Jesus, now King and about to unleash His wrath, is still our Intercessor to the last. He continues to pray to the Father just as He did in the Garden of Gethsemane. His heart is crying out, "Is there no other way? Must they be lost forever? Oh, Father, the lashings, the crown of thorns, the nails in My hands and feet were nothing to the agony I now feel!" (See Matthew 26:36-45.)

Turn to the Lord

During the reign of Darius in the sixth century B.C., the people of Israel experienced both emotional stress and physical affliction. They had been relentlessly overrun by surrounding enemies, yet apparently no one had the presence of mind to address the causes. Or, more likely, they tried to find solutions to spiritual problems on the level of human reasoning.

God sent the prophet Zechariah with a message for them: If they would turn back to Him, He promised to restore their peace and prosperity. (See Book of Zechariah.) God's unending love for His people continues to prevail. Today, we are still trying to find human solutions such as communism, psychology, child-raising, restructured public education, and New Age philosophies. Today, as then, God continues to urge all nations to turn back to Him.

He loves the nations of the world to the same degree that He loves you and me, and He details His promises in Zechariah 10. I have substituted the name "Hopi" for the names "Israel" and "Judah" in order to personalize the message to the Hopi people. I urge you to substitute the name of the individual, people group, or mission field that God has placed on your heart.

Zechariah Chapter 10

> Ask the Lord for rain in the springtime, and He will answer with lightning and showers. Every field will become a lush pasture. How foolish to ask the idols [misconceived "sacred" beings] for anything like that! Fortune-tellers' [sorcerers'] predictions are all

a bunch of silly lies; what comfort is there in promises that don't come true? [The Hopi] have been led astray and wander like lost sheep; everyone attacks them, for they have a shepherd [Jesus Christ] to protect them.

I will strengthen [the Hopi]; I will establish them because I love them.

Their children, too, shall see the mercies of the Lord and be glad. Their hearts shall rejoice in the Lord...From the few that are left, their population will grow again to former size.

The Lord says, "I will make [the Hopi] strong with power from me" (author's paraphrase of Zechariah 10:1-8).

In Zechariah chapter 13 God promises that in the end:

...a Fountain [or Spring, which is Jesus Christ] will be opened to [the Hopi people], a Fountain to cleanse them from all their sins and uncleanness.

...In that day I will get rid of every vestige of idol worship throughout the land, so that even the names of the idols will be forgotten. All the false prophets and fortune-tellers [sorcerers] will be wiped out...

No one will be boasting then of his prophetic gift...No, he will say, I am not a prophet; I am a [Hopi] farmer. The soil has been my livelihood from my earliest youth (author's paraphrase of Zechariah 13:1-5).

Chapter 9

A Vindication and Apology

Jesus said: "I have many things to speak and to judge concerning you, but He who sent Me is true; and the things which I heard from Him, these I speak to the world...If you abide in My word, then you are truly disciples of Mine; and you shall know the truth, and the truth shall make you free" (John 8:26-32).

God's Truth sets men and women free. This means that wrongs must be righted and unholy things must be purified by His Truth. Although the evangelist cannot change the past, he can acknowledge the dark deeds of the past and expose them to the Light of Jesus Christ. If public apologies are called for, they can and should be given.

Unspeakable acts have been perpetrated upon the people throughout history, ostensibly in the name of God and the Cross. The acts were evil, but it is the enemy (satan) that we must hate. He is the appropriate target for our righteous indignation.

Religious atrocities occurred throughout world history, from the earliest Christian persecution during the lifetime

Evangelizing the Culturally Different

of Jesus to the horrors facing the New Testament believers and later the Christian Crusades. The inhuman treatment of God's people during the Jewish Holocaust and the shameful conditions perpetuated by American slavery are still alive in the hearts of men and women everywhere. Ignorant men justified their actions in the name of God and hid behind the walls of antiseptic church walls and government institutions.

We gasp in horror at their crimes, but the truth is, in another time and place, you or I might have been numbered among the persecutors. Today we have the tremendous benefit of historical research, Bible criticism, media news, and the flood of information at our fingertips. Years ago, a less informed world allowed these early religious leaders to "give the devil opportunity."

Indian Persecutions

The Native American Indians have suffered the indignations of ignorance since the time that the white men stepped foot upon their land. The seventeenth-century Franciscan padres carried out their *regula* (official orders from the king) with Old Testament brutality. Threats of punishment kept the Indians under enforced conformity.

Some of the Indians were hung by the arms and whipped. Others were forced to stand in a small circle for hours at a time on public display. A few were hung. A Hopi's hair was a symbol of personal worth: It was a common practice to cut the "rebel's" hair.[1]

In 1661, royal troops on orders from the padres raided the *kivas*, seized 1,600 *kachina* masks (objects as holy to the Hopi as temple utensils were to the ancient Jews), and burned them.[2] In the 1930's, the indomitable Elsie Clews

A Vindication and Apology

Parson (an anthropologist, social reformer, and journalist) burst into *kiva* ceremonies quite uninvited to disturb and contaminate holy rituals.

These things happened a long time ago, but the Hopi haven't forgotten them any more than our African-Americans have forgotten slavery or the Jewish people have forgotten Hitler's inhumanity. In addition to the wretched treatment and self-interest policies of our American government, Christian missionaries also have produced pain and animosity among the Hopi people.

The Crime of Ignorance Has Many Faces

In general, today's saints are answering a definite calling from the Lord and lack no dedication to the tenets of the full gospel. They know that to love their neighbor is to love God. Yet Christians often overlook the denominational schisms and petty differences between factions of the Christian church (not to mention cults that use the name of Christ). It goes without saying that a non-believer has little means to sort out truth from falsehood, particularly when a Catholic, Protestant, or cult member presents himself as a representative of the gospel and then proceeds to "knock the competition."

Undoubtedly, the evangelist would be shocked and hurt to discover that his work in the field has been considered offensive. Herein lies the tragedy. The *offense* to which I refer is one of "omission, a lack of preparation, and a failure to learn the cultural distinctions."

Christians, "whose hearts are in the right place," often assume that all they need is the gospel to challenge and convert others whose ideas are very different from their own.

They seem to think they don't need to know anything about the culture they wish to work in.

God's Word tells us to prepare ourselves for the task: "Study to shew thyself approved unto God, a workman that needeth not to be ashamed, rightly dividing the word of truth" (2 Tim. 2:15 KJV). I do not believe this passage refers to simply memorizing the Bible, but also includes knowing how and when to apply God's Word for Kingdom Culture Evangelism.

In an extreme situation, I do not have the slightest doubt that the Lord will provide everything we need. But He expects something from us too! The Christian's walk is conditional and cooperative: "If you...then, I will...." The expectation that the Lord will provide all, and that the evangelist does not need to study or prepare, is both naive and unscriptural. The amount of preparation undertaken by the mighty saints such as Moses, Joshua, and Paul is nothing short of astounding.

Careless Words Cause Our Brothers to Stumble

For the lips of a priest should preserve knowledge, and men should seek instruction from his mouth; for he is the messenger of the Lord of hosts. But as for you, you have turned aside from the way; you have caused many to stumble by the instruction; you have corrupted the covenant... (Malachi 2:7-8).

Many missionaries and Christian workers have innocently called all Hopi religious practices "satanic." This has been disastrous to the Hopi people and a heavy weight to the gospel. It has kept many godly Hopi people from fully accepting God's Truth.

A Vindication and Apology

Literary scholars often have suggested that if Plato had only known Jesus, he would have been one of the world's greatest Christian teachers. I feel much the same way about some of the great Hopi leaders of the past and present. The village chiefs, *kikmongwis*, and other leaders (many of whom are women) are called "Wise Ones" for a very good reason. They are wise, not only in folk wisdom, but also in intellect and spirit. They are living monuments to God's mercy, grace, and determination—monuments showing that His creation knows Him.

Yet I have heard pastors, teachers, and other missionaries speak about the "devil's drums," "ungodly masked dancers," and "devil dances" on numerous occasions. My heart was grieved when I heard these things.

In contrast to the alleged presence of satan at Hopi ceremonies, I assert that God's Spirit is omnipresent. A Hopi elder once informed me that the purpose of all dances is to bring rain to Hopiland in order to insure a good crop of corn—the basis of Hopi diet. I have never attended a single dance that did not result in generous amounts. I need not point out to Christians that satan is not so faithful nor so concerned with human needs. At the end of the last dance I attended, in addition to a downpour, a brilliant rainbow arched the sky from horizon to horizon at the ceremony's conclusion. I took this rainbow as a reminder from the Lord that never again would He cover the earth with water (see Gen. 9:12-17).

An Apology to the Hopi People

Are you serving in a place or among a people group who deserves a sincere apology for past offenses? You do not need to travel to a alien culture to meet wounded people who stand in need of God's unconditional love. Some of our churches are filled with Christians who still remember past offenses of "omission, a lack of preparation, and a failure to learn basic denominational distinctions." If you are, be generous. Extend an apology not only for your own lack, but also for those that have walked in their lives before you:

If therefore there is any encouragement in Christ, if there is any consolation of love, if there is any fellowship of the Spirit, if any affection and compassion, make my joy complete by being of the same mind, maintaining the same love, united in spirit, intent on one purpose. Do nothing from selfishness or empty conceit, but with humility of mind let each of you regard one another as more important than himself; do not merely look out for your own personal interests, but also for the interests of others. Have this attitude in yourselves which was also in Christ Jesus... (Philippians 2:1-5).

If we say that we have no sin, we are deceiving ourselves, and the truth is not in us. If we confess our sins, He is faithful and righteous to forgive us our sins and to cleanse us from all unrighteousness (1 John 1:8-9).

I would like to take this opportunity to extend a public apology to the Hopi people, which also can be used as an outline of reference for your own mission field, be it near or far away:

My dear Hopi brothers and sisters, on behalf of all misguided or misinformed representatives of the Gospel of Jesus Christ and in His Holy Name, I repent of our sin against you. We have sinned against you by leaning on our own knowledge and not the full gospel, both in the past and in the present.

Over the years, in our ignorance, we have committed heinous crimes against you, and I ask your forgiveness. I pray for a reunion of spirit as brothers and sisters in Christ. We love you, even though from time to time we have been spiritually foolish. Let us join together as we search for God, the Author of Truth.

Trust the Holy Spirit

United with one another, we must trust the Holy Spirit. Jesus sent Him to be our guide (see Jn. 14:16-17). It is my firm belief that the evangelist's work does not consist in undermining native beliefs or religious systems. This is not what Jesus sent the Holy Spirit to do. Instead, the Holy Spirit empowers us to spread the Good News of the gospel. When a conversion is complete, the Holy Spirit will eliminate all the false doctrine *in His own time and in His own way!*

God's written Word reveals God's Truth and transforms the hearts and lives of converts. The evangelist is not going to change anyone's mind. This is the work of the Holy Spirit. He alone has the power to create new creatures in Christ:

Therefore if any man is in Christ, he is a new creature; the old things passed away; behold, new things have come. Now all these things are from God, who reconciled us to Himself through Christ, and gave us the ministry of reconciliation, namely, that God was in Christ reconciling the world to Himself, not counting their trespasses against them, and He has committed to us the word of reconciliation. Therefore, we are ambassadors for Christ, as though God were entreating through us, we beg you on behalf of Christ, be reconciled to God (2 Corinthians 5:17-20).

Chapter 10

Pray for the Nations

Ask of Me, and I will surely give the nations as Thine inheritance, and the very ends of the earth as Thy possession (Psalm 2:8).

God is still claiming the nations for His Son, Jesus. "A sower went forth to sow" ought to be the picture of the Christian world today. Jesus Christ is the sower, and the Word of God is the seed. Today, we also have a commission. We are not directed to harvest, which is the work of the Holy Spirit. We are urged to sow, sow, sow! We are His arm extended; we are to keep sowing for Him (see Lk. 8:4-15 and Rev. 14:14-15).

Guard Against Personal Prejudice

Cross-cultural awareness has increased in recent times. However, hurtful preconceived ideas and deep-seated (often hidden) personal prejudices are still a part of man's sinful nature. Believers are not exempt, so we must guard against these with prayer and study. Whenever an evangelist in the field finds himself faced with a circumstance that offends him personally, he must profoundly, at length, question himself as to the reason for his offense.

Evangelizing the Culturally Different

Pray, search the Scriptures, and get acquainted with native views regarding the object of offense. His views may very widely from your own conclusions. In the end, the only conclusion that has legitimacy is God's. The variety in His creation is amazing and wonderful. God's ways are not our ways, and His thoughts are not our thoughts (see Is. 55:9). In addition God works within His own time-frame.

Bridge the Gap and Wage Victory

In First Timothy chapter two Paul urges believers to offer requests, prayers, intercession, and thanksgiving on behalf of all men (especially those in authority), so that all people may lead peaceful and quiet lives, full of godliness and dignity (see 1 Tim. 2:1-2). Unmistakenly, the Bible places a high priority upon prayer for those in authority.

This exhortation prompts all Christians to pray not only for our own leaders but also for the leaders of other nations. Our personal feelings should not be our guide, for "...there is no [governing] authority except from God..." (Rom. 13:1). The Scriptures establish the fact that governing authorities are established by God and that a Christian should give them prayerful support. God is sovereign over all mankind, and He arranges the affairs of all nations according to His divinely ordained plan.

This assures us that the present events of a nation have meaning insofar as they contribute to God's ultimate design. Virtually nothing happens by accident. Spiritual, economic, political, and all other forces come together, conforming to God's sovereign will. Hopiland is an excellent example of this.

Pray for Hopiland

Prayer should be directed specifically toward common beliefs and the formulation of policies that will provide peace, stability, and a thorough understanding of God's salvation. As you conclude this book, I ask you to pray for Hopiland. The following summary of trends in Hopiland today will help you to understand and pray for specific issues.

Three major trends exist in Hopiland that form the framework that the Hopi will use to make decisions concerning their future. First, a generation of young people has been educated by mainstream public school education. The objectives are often in conflict with traditional Hopi goals and often are mutually exclusive of them—a consequence that brings about a generation gap causing "psychological cacophony" within both generations. The older generation espouses the Hopi Way, while mainstream public education espouses humanism. Tragically, neither offers a full-gospel world view. Happily, Christianity offers the solution: Christ is the Great Mediator between the two. He is "the Way, the Truth, and the Light" (see Jn. 14:6).

A second major trend among the Hopi is a move from regionalism, which also threatens the traditional way of life, while embracing the mainstream American worldview. As one would expect, religious rivalries and ideological disputes constitute a destabilizing factor. One hopes that this schism will not lead to a replay of the "hostiles and friendlies" civil war. Jesus Christ provides both the answer and the solution.

A third factor is the contemporary Hopi's response to economic challenges. With the breakdown of the traditional way of life, i.e. corn-planting and corn-grinding, off-reservation jobs have become a fact of Hopi life, resulting in alcohol consumption and alcoholism. Away-jobs require away-living arrangements, both of which upset the ceremonial cycle. Some ritual preparations and performances demand the physical presence of specific members of the clan society involved.

During the last few years, certain ceremonies have been planned to end on a weekend, thus allowing away-job holders to come home for participation in the public dances. I have learned that the mandated purification rites for a particular ceremonial participant sometimes must be truncated. Or sometimes ceremonies have to be performed by a substitute, thereby jeopardizing the effectiveness of the ceremony.

There is reason for optimism regarding the Hopi future. Among the younger generation are individuals aware of U.S. national citizenship as well as their own ethnic identity. Yet the pressure from traditionalists remains because they fear the loss of the very Hopi philosophy that informs and instructs the Hopi mind.

Knowledgeable missionaries, teachers, and other Christians should use the Hopi Way as common ground to share the gospel and as a bridge to carry the hope of salvation to Hopi who do not have clear proof and an understanding of it. What a blessed cargo to transport, and what a sanctified bridge to cross and recross! No matter how different the cultures may seem to be, common values do exist and pertinent topics of genuine mutual interest always offer opportunity for dialogue.

All People Need the Lord

Regardless of our mission field, there are four vital points to keep in mind when looking for ways to touch people's hearts. These have been gleaned from a teaching presented by my own pastor, Dr. Paul C. Risser. They represent the key elements of a Kingdom Culture.

All people need the Lord. "...The righteousness of God through faith in Jesus Christ [is] for all those who believe; for there is no distinction; for all have sinned and fall short of the glory of God..." (see Rom. 3:22-23).

The Holy Spirit has preceded you and has been preparing their hearts to receive Jesus. You are not the first one to come. Jesus said, "No one can come to Me, unless the Father [Holy Spirit] who sent Me draws him..." (see Jn 6:44).

God has a plan for everyone to be saved. Second Peter 3:9 says, "[He is] not wishing for any to perish but for all to come to repentance."

We must understand our role in God's plan. We are sent to proclaim the gospel in the context of a Kingdom Culture. Jesus did not send us to *culturalize* but to *evangelize* (see Mt. 28:19-20).

God puts us in the right place at the right time. Let us be prepared to lovingly deal with those He puts into our path.

Endnotes

Acknowledgments

1. Mary Ann Lind, *Asia: A Christian Perspective* (Seattle, Washington: Frontline Communications, 1970), p. ix.

Preface

1. Harold E. Driver, *Indians of North America* (Chicago: The University of Chicago Press, 1961), p. 17.

2. Lind, p. 121.

3. Lind, p. 121.

Introduction

1. Lind, p. 12

2. T.S. Eliot, "The Art of Literary Research," in *A Handbook of Critical Approaches to Literature* (New York: Harper and Row, 1975), p. 5.

3. Harry C. James, *Pages From Hopi History* (Tucson, Arizona: The University of Arizona Press, 1977), p. xi.

Chapter 1

1. John D. Loftin, *Religion and Hopi Life in the Twentieth Century* (Bloomington, Indiana: Indiana University Press, 1991), p. 25.

2. Loftin, p. 25.

3. Albert Yava and Harold Courlander, *Big Falling Snow: A Tewa-Hopi Indian's Life and Times and the History and Traditions of His Hopi People* (New York: Crown Publishers, Inc., 1978), p. 165.

Chapter 2

1. Arrell Morgan Gibson, *The American Indian: Prehistory to the Present* (Lexington, Massachusetts: D.C. Heath and Company, 1980), p. 105.

2. Harry C. James, *Pages From Hopi History* (Tucson, Arizona: The University of Arizona Press, 1979), p. 54.

3. Charles Wilson Hackett, *The Revolt of the Pueblo Indians of New Mexico and Otermin's Attempted Reconquest, 1690-1692,* (Albuquerque, New Mexico: University of New Mexico Press, 1942), p. 100.

4. James, p.85.

5. Helen Sekawquaptewa, *Me and Mine* (Tucson, Arizona: The University of Arizona Press, 1977), p. 235.

6. James, p. 130-192, and in other accounts.

7. James, p. 136.

8. James, p. 146.

9. Yava, p. 26.

10. Marion E. Herd, *Treasures of Darkness,* Unpublished journals, letters, and poems; 1988-1992.

11. Elisabeth Q. White, *No Turning Back* (Albuquerque, New Mexico: University of New Mexico Press, 1981), p. 14.

12. George Otis, Jr., *The Last of the Giants* (Tarrytown, New York: Fleming H. Revell Company, 1991), p. 261.

13. James, p. 85.

Chapter 3

1. George Sayer, *Jack: A Life of C.S. Lewis* (Wheaton, Illinois: Crossways Books, 1994), p. 225.

2. Sayer, p. 225.

3. Loftin, p.14.

4. C.S. Lewis, *The Pilgrim's Regress* (London: William B. Eerdman's Publishing Company, 1943), p. 198.

5. Frank Waters, *Book of the Hopi* (New York: The Viking Press, 1969), p. 3.

Chapter 4

1. James A. Michener, *Hawaii* (New York: Bantam Books, Inc., 1959), p. 320.

2. Mischa Titiev, *Old Oraibi: A Study of the Hopi Indians of Third Mesa* Vol. 22, No. 1 (Cambridge, Massachusetts: Harvard University Press, 1944), p. 55 and 273.

3. F. Eggan, *Social Organization of the Western Pueblos* (Chicago: University of Chicago Press, 1933), p. 63.

4. Leo W. Simmons, Ed., *Sun Chief: The Autobiography of a Hopi Indian* (New Haven: Yale University Press, 1963), p. 18.

5. Louis Hieb, *Masks and Meaning: A Contextual Approach to the Hopi Tuvi'ku* (Careeley, Colorado: University of Northern Colorado Museum of Anthropology, 1979), p. 65.

6. C.S. Lewis, *Christian Reflections* (Grand Rapids, Michigan: William B. Eerdman's Publishing Company, 1967), p. 44.

7. Mando Sevillano, *Overcoming Blue Eyes* (Huntington, West Virginia: Aegina Press, Inc., 1988), p. 34.

8. Barton Wright, *The Year of the Hopi* (Baltimore: Smithsonian Institution Service, 1979), p. 17.

Evangelizing the Culturally Different

9. Simmons, p. 18.

10. Simmons, p. 18.

Chapter 5

1. Margaret Mead, *Growing Up in New Guinea* (New York: The New American Library, 1953), p. 115.

2. Mando Sevillano, *The Hopi Way: Tales From A Changing Culture* (Flagstaff, Arizona: Northland Publishing, 1986), p. 55.

3. Driver, p. 5.

4. Driver, p. 5.

Chapter 6

1. Watchman Nee, *Song of Songs* (Fort Washington, Pennsylvania: Christian Literature Crusade, 1989), p. 43.

Chapter 7

1. Lind, p. 182.

Chapter 8

1. C.S. Lewis, *Reflections on the Psalms* (San Diego: Harcourt, Brace and Company, 1986), p. 36.

2. Lewis, p. 36.

3. Samuel Enoch Stumpt, ed., *Socrates To Sarte: A History of Philosophy* (San Francisco: McGraw-Hill Book Company, 1975), p. 67.

4. Stumpt, p.37.

5. Lewis, p. 110.

Chapter 9

1. Gibson, p. 103.

2. Gibson, p. 103.

Appendix: Reliable and Accessible Hopi Stories

Be diligent to present yourself approved to God as a workman who does not need to be ashamed, handling accurately the word of truth (2 Timothy 2:15).

One must learn to distinguish authentic sacred Hopi stories (also called myths, legends, or tales) because many commercially-minded people have retold and reworked authentic materials for their own purposes. Although many commercial versions (most often arranged for an audience of children) are charming and valuable for teaching good morals in a general way, they often lack the authority of original intent— divine admonition, exhortation, edification, and observation. Stories told by a Hopi or recorded by a Hopi (with or without assistance) are reliable. The variation from teller to teller is quite analogous with the variations we find in the numerous translations of the Bible. Some other collections of stories are also reliable, but a bit of research may be warranted to determine their reliability.

The diligent student will see parallels to well-known Bible stories. *Fieldmouse Goes to War,* for example, is a clear echo of of David and Goliath. I recommend the following stories and collections of stories.

Especially for Children

Fieldmouse Goes to War: Tusan Homichi Tuwvota. Told by Albert Yava, recorded by Edward A. Kennard. Illustrations by Fred Kabotie (one of the most famous Hopi artists). Palmer Lake, Colorado: The Filter Press, 1977. Albert Yava is a Tewa-Hopi elder, well-versed in traditional knowledge.

Hopi Bride at the Home Dance and Other Stories. Anthony Honahnie, Alfonso Sekewa, and Terrence Talaswaima. Washington, D.C.: The Hopi Action Program, 1977. All contributors are Hopi storytellers and artists of the first rank. Other stories included in the book are "The Eagle Hunt," "Winter Rabbit Hunter," and "The Birds of Hano Village."

For All Ages

Gullible Coyote: Una'hu. Malotko and Lomatuway'ma. Here are a dozen stories of Coyote, the "Trickster," whose behavior often is devilish. Coyote, although rebellious against accepted standards of proper behavior, is not the exact counterpart of satan. He is merely foolish. In the Hopi Way, Coyote teaches by negative example.

Hopitutuwutsi: Hopi Tales (A Bilingual Collection of Hopi Indian Stories). Please refer to the Bibliography for complete documentation.

Stories of Maasaw, a Hopi God by Ekkehart Malotki and Michael Lomatuway'ma. This includes sixteen stories of a fascinating, fearsome, sacred being. The authors use of the term "god" is somewhat misleading: the Hopi people believe

Appendix

in one Creator God. Other sacred beings have been called "gods" by outsiders so long and so relentlessly that even contemporary Hopi tend to use the term in the same way. Please refer to the Bibliography for complete documentation.

Spider Woman Stories: Legends of the Hopi Indian. G.M. Mullett. Tucson: The University of Arizona Press, 1979. Although these eleven stories were not collected by a Hopi, they have been scrutinized by reputable scholars in the field of Hopi studies and the Hopi people have not rejected them. These stories give insight into the Hopi female character and female aspects of the creation. According to the Hopi Way, Spider Woman (also called Spider Grandmother) is the sacred being who created humans.

The Hopi Way: Tales of a Changing Culture. The first printing of this book carried the subtitle "Tales of a Vanishing Culture." Seven teaching stories were collected from Hopi storytellers and were translated into English by a Hopi elder, assisted by the author. Please refer to the Bibliography for complete documentation.

Bibliography

American Bible Society of New York, ed. (1972) *God Lavayiyat An Puhuvasiwni*. New York.

Christie, George V., ed. (1949) *Pictorial America: Arizona Edition*. Phoenix, Arizona: First National Bank of Arizona. (Cover photo by Ray J. Manley).

Courlander, Harold. (1971) *The Fourth World of the Hopis*. Greenwich, New York: Fawcett Publications, Inc.

Cutler, Mike. (1995) " God's Work" in *American Indian Culture and Research Journal*, Vol. 19, No. 1, p. 192.

Eggan, F. (1933) *Social Organization of the Wester Pueblos*. Chicago: University of Chicago Press.

Driver, Harold E. (1961) *Indians of North America*. Chicago: The University of Chicago Press.

Geertz, Armin W. and Michael Lomatuway'ma. (1987) *Children of Cottonwood: Piety and Ceremonialism in Hopi Indian Puppetry*. Lincoln, Nebraska: University of Nebraska Press.

Gibson, Arrell Morgan. (1980) *The American Indian: Prehistory to the Present*. Lexington, Massachusetts: D.C. Heath and Company.

Herd, Marion E. (1988-1992) " Treasures of Darkness," Unpublished journals, letters, and poems.

Hieb, Louis. (1979) "Masks and Meaning: A Contextual Approach to the Hopi Tuvi'ku." Greeley, Colorado: University of Northern Colorado Museum of Anthropology.

James, Harry C. (1979) *Pages from Hopi History*. Tucson, Arizona: The University of Arizona Press.

Laird, David C. (1977) *Hopi Bibliography*. Tucson, Arizona: The University of Arizona Press.

Lewis, C.S. (1967) *Christian Reflections*. Grand Rapids: William B. Eerdmans Publishing Company.

_____. (1943) *Mere Christianity*. New York: MacMillan Publishing Co., Inc.

_____. (1986) *Reflections on the Psalms*. San Diego: Harcourt, Brace & Company.

_____. (1943) *The Pilgrim's Regress*. London: William B. Eerdman's Publishing Co.

Lind, Mary Ann. (1970) *Asia: A Christian Perspective*. Seattle, Washington: Frontline Communications.

Loftin, John D. (1991) *Religion and Hopi Life in the Twentieth Century*. Bloomington: Indiana University Press.

Malotki, Ekkehart. (1985) *Gullible Coyote: Una'hu*. Tucson, Arizona: The University of Arizona Press.

_____. (1978) *Hopitutuwutsi: Hopi Tales (A Bilingual Collection of Hopi Indian Stories)*. Flagstaff, Arizona: Museum of Northern Arizona Press.

Malotki, Ekkehart and Michael Lomatuway'ma. (1987) *Massaw: Profile of a Hopi God*. Lincoln, Nebraska: University of Nebraska Press.

_____. (1987) *Stories of Massaw, A Hopi God*. Lincoln, Nebraska: University of Nebraska Press.

Mead, Margaret. (1953) *Growing Up in New Guinea*. New York: The New American Library.

Michener, James A. (1959) *Hawaii*. New York: Bantam Books.

McDonald, George. (1984)*The Musician's Quest*. Mineapolis: Bethany House Publishers.

Nee, Watchman. (1965) *Song of Songs*. Fort Washington, Pennsylvania: Christian Literature Crusade.

O'Kane, Walter. (1950) *The Hopis: Portrait of a Desert People*. Norman, Oklahoma: University of Oklahoma Press.

Otis, George, Jr. (1991) *The Last of the Giants: Lifting the Veil of Islam and the End Times*. Tarrytown, New York: Fleming H. Revell Co.

Phillips, Michael R. (1987) *George MacDonald: Scotland's Beloved Storyteller*. Minneapolis: Bethany House Publishers.

Qoyawayma, Polingaysi (Elisabeth Q. White). (1964) *No Turning Back: A Hopi Indian Woman's Struggle to Live in Two Worlds*. Albuquerque, New Mexico: The University of New Mexico Press.

Sayer, George. (1994) *Jack: A Life of C.S. Lewis*. Wheaton, Illinois: Crossways Books.

Sekaquapetwa, Helen. (1977) *Me and Mine: The Life of Helen Sekaquapetwa*. Tucson, Arizona: University of Arizona Press.

Sevillano, Mando. (1986) *The Hopi Way: Tales from a Changing Culture*. Flagstaff, Arizona: Northland Publishing.

_____ . (1986) "Interpreting Native American Literature: An Archetpal Approach" in *American Indian Culture and Research Journal*. Vol. 10, No. 1.

_____ . (1988) *Overcoming Clue Eyes*. Huntington, West Virginia: Aegina Press, Inc.

Simmons, Leo W., ed. (1963) *Sun Chief: The Autobiography of a Hopi Indian.* New Haven, Connecticut: Yale University Press.

Stewart, Tyrone and others. (1981) *The Year of the Hopi.* Washington D.C.: Smithsonian Institution Traveling Exhibition Service.

Stumpt, Samuel Enoch. (1975) *Socrates to Sartre: A History of Philosophy.* San Francisco: McGraw-Hill Book Company.

Titiev, Misch. (1933) *Old Oraibi: A Study of the Hopi Indians of Third Mesa.* Vol. 22, No. 1. Chicago. University of Chicago Press.

Udall, Louise. (1977) *Me and Mine: The Story of Helen Sekaquaptewa.* Tucson, Arizona: The University of Arizona Press.

Walters, Anna Lee. (1988) *Ghost Singer.* Flagstaff, Arizona: Northland Publishing.

Waters, Frank. (1963) *Book of the Hopi.* New York: The Viking Press.

_____. (1950) *Masked Gods: Navaho and Pueblo Ceremonialism.* New York: Ballantine Books.

_____. (1973) *Pumpkin Seed Point: Being Within the Hopi.* Chicago: The Swallow Press.

Wright, Barton. (1979) *The Year of the Hopi.* Baltimore: Smithsonian Institution Service

Yava, Albert and Harold Courlander. (1978) *Big Falling Snow: A Tewa-Hopi Indian's Life and Times and the History and Traditions of His Hopi People.* New York: Crown Publishers, Inc.

Other *exciting titles*

UNDERSTANDING THE DIFFICULT WORDS OF JESUS
by David Bivin and Roy Blizzard, Jr.
This book clearly describes ways of understanding some original Hebrew and Greek techniques and of discovering the true meanings of many of the words of Jesus. This book will be an important addition to your personal or group Bible study time. *Newly Revised!*
Paperback Book, 160p. ISBN 1-56043-550-X Retail $9.99

THE SECRET OF SOUL-WINNING
by Stephen F. Olford.
Billy Graham calls Stephen F. Olford "one of the most successful soul-winners I have ever met." Being sensitive to the direction of the Holy Spirit is the key to consistent effective witnessing. Men and women alike are prepared by the Lord for spreading the gospel. This book will help you respond to the Lord and reap the harvest.
Paperback Book, 126p. ISBN 1-56043-800-2 Retail $7.99

ANOINTING THE UNSANCTIFIED
by Dr. Mark Hanby.
The anointing is more than a talented performance or an emotional response. In this book, Dr. Hanby details the essential ingredients of directional relationship that allow the Spirit of God to flow down upon the Body of Christ—and from us to the needs of a dying world.
Paperback Book, 196p. ISBN 1-56043-071-0 Retail $8.99

Available at your local Christian bookstore.

Internet: http://www.reapernet.com

Prices subject to change without notice.

Other *exciting titles*

GROWING IN CHRISTIAN MATURITY
by Herman Riffel.
Author Herman Riffel illustrates the power of inner healing and the great release that comes to troubled souls, and touches on the many ways God speaks to us. This book shows what tremendous power has been given to God's sons and daughters and describes the true manifestations of His gifts to us. Discover what God can do through and for humanity! (Previously published as *Christian Maturity.*)
Paperback Book, 210p. ISBN 1-56043-191-1 Retail $8.99

DIDN'T YOU READ MY BOOK?
by Dr. Richard E. Eby.
This best-selling book is a provocative look at the truths to be found in God's book, written by one who has seen the reality of many of these truths for himself. Dr. Eby has said, "The best possible experience on earth is to converse with Almighty God; the next best is to share His words with others; and third best is to have a reader who is open to hear His truth."
Paperback Book, 170p. ISBN 1-56043-448-1 Retail $7.99

FROM MILK TO MEAT
by Bishop Arthur M. Brazier.
Have you ever wondered how you can live a Christian life in the midst of the chaotic and violent society we have today? This book provides a strong foundation for studying basic beliefs and practices of the Christian life. Don't miss this opportunity to become a living example of Christ in your community!
Paperback Book, 126p. ISBN 1-56043-278-0 Retail $6.99

Available at your local Christian bookstore.

Internet: http://www.reapernet.com

Prices subject to change without notice.